MAURO BERNO

LEAD THE WAY

THE MODERN APPROACH TO GROWING
YOUR BUSINESS IN THE DIGITAL AGE

LEAD THE WAY

THE MODERN APPROACH TO GROWING YOUR BUSINESS IN THE DIGITAL AGE

MAURO BERNO

AUTHOR'S NOTE

SECTION ONE: MARKETING

SECTION TWO: SALES

AUTHOR'S NOTE

Marketing and sales have changed a lot in the last 20 years as digital technology has gone from the realm of the scientific and the academic to commonplace for virtually every industry and business on earth. What was once the arena of much educated guesswork as to why customers were buying a certain product or how effective a radio ad, television commercial, or newspaper circular were is now trackable in 20 different ways thanks to a litany of new gadgets and inventions that seem to grow at an exponential rate from week to week. Clicks, views, opens, impressions, heat maps, and more now drive decision-making; gut feelings and playing your hunches seem to have been relegated to the storage closet.

But lost in the shuffle of being the first company in your industry to integrate and start delivering results with all these new technological triumphs is a mislaid truth about the way business is done.

In May 2017, the highly-regarded publication The Economist shook up the world landscape with a cover piece declaring that data had replaced oil as the world's most valuable resource. For many industries, this has become their new normal. Pulling in as many bits of data from as many touch points as possible, feeding them all into engines driven by Machine Learning, and gleaning the results to drive every future business decision is the standard, not the exception. Marketing departments around the world have jumped on the digital technology wave like the world's most skilled surfers, engaging it for insights on their customers, as close to real-time as possible. Some firms are pushing the frontier even harder, enabling Artificial Intelligence components to begin writing sales and marketing copy and even actual content for themselves and their clients. Give enough data, they say, and at some point a general audience won't know if an ad was written by a human hand or a digital one. Many marketing firms and departments are feasting on all this data and analytics that come with it. They can throw off the shackles of some of the routine tasks that were devouring too much of their time. Now all they have to do is click a few buttons, toggle a few switches, implement the suggestions, and away we go.

But that's where they're wrong, and where the Economist's bold proclamation of three years ago meets its match. The rest of the world might be ga-ga for Big Data and its powers of pattern-finding and extrapolation but there's a commodity out there that dwarfs all the numbers in the world: People.

No piece of data has ever bought a product, had a change of heart, or committed to a brand for life. Every brand's customers are attracted to marketing because it expresses the firm's essence and identity.

AI, advanced analytics, Big Data, and all the rest of the impressive technology spectrum currently spreading like wildfire across the world are not the answer to your marketing question, but rather the tools that help marketers identify, create, and target in formats that save time, money, and manpower.

For marketers, the addition of these tools is like spending years trying to build the Great Wall of China with pickaxes and shovels, and suddenly one day a fleet of 5,000 cranes and bulldozers arrives. The technology makes the job quicker and easier, but the people at the heart of it are still the ones building the wall.

Focusing all your efforts on your customers is a strategy known as relationship marketing. It means that everything you are doing is to develop strong, life-long customers. If you do it correctly, not only will you attract more customers, but you will also retain more of the existing ones. Researchers find that a 1% increase in customer retention in a year equates to a 20% increase in a company's annual revenue. The most important part of relationship marketing is facilitating two-way conversations with customers, which satiates desires of both company and consumer. This personal touch and aligned service is a much larger part of successful sales and marketing than anything done by AI or the rest of the digital revolution. In this book we will explore the role of sales and marketing in the modern business environment and focus on a strategy that is customer-centric and people driven rather than analytical and data-driven.

SECTION ONE: MARKETING

DON'T BE AFRAID TO GET CREATIVE AND EXPERIMENT WITH YOUR MARKETING.

Mike Volpe

CHAPTER 1

WHY MARKETING AND SALES ALIGNMENT MATTERS

WHAT IS MBS?

MBS is a term that will be frequently used in this book. It is an acronym for Marketing, Buyer, and Sales, a three-pronged relationship that is at the heart of shifting a company's focus from data to people. You can imagine these three terms as a letter X with one leg as Marketing, the other as Sales and the Buyer as the spot where the two of them intersect. We position the Buyer in the center between our Marketing strategy and our Sales plan, as both must act harmoniously to give the customer the best possible experience.

WHY FOCUS ON MBS?

Selling your products and services is a lot different than it was as recently as 15 years ago. It has not just been technology changing the game, although that certainly has played a major role. The movements of the economy - both globally and domestically - as well as customers themselves. They have gained a propensity to want tailor-made experiences that cater to their individual needs rather than buying generic products and bending their own goals to those of the corporations. Customer expectations have never been higher.

In the industries, products and services have become commodified. Competition has become fiercer then ever with the rise of small businesses as well as online businesses and e-commerce. Twenty years ago if you wanted to set up a store, you needed a brick-and-mortar location, all sorts of government approval for taxes and fees, staff to work the store, money for utilities, etc. Now, an online business can be set up in a matter of minutes by anyone with an Internet connection and a place to store the product, and now often without storage with a drop-shipping model. This produces hyper-competition, where businesses will undercut each other to an extreme simply to be the firm that gets the order, but doing business at that price can never be sustained.

Technology also warps consumers' emotional responses through the use of social media, fake news, and planted reviews. Customer fickleness - a scenario that develops when customers have too much information and too many choices - to know how to make a logical decision, is another fall out of how loud and up close the world can be through digital technology.

So much noise means even the most competent of marketing professionals can see their efforts be classified as just another dull buzz in the minds of their target audiences. Opening up those critical dialogues with our customers is a delicate process that takes real emotion and willingness to connect. Believing that our hard skills alone, things like product knowledge, goal-setting, industry-specific skills and CRM software management will win through to the end is not realistic.

Just as marketing has changed, so too has sales. Two decades ago, sales and marketing were siloed entities of the same business corporation, with each having its own agenda, plans, and ways of measuring results. Today, sales is part of the wider mix that embodies relationship marketing, and marketing is an accountable part of the sales process. This change is largely due to two reasons: 1) Consumer habits have dramatically changed and 2) Old standard sales techniques no longer work.

Both of those reasons are impacted largely by the Internet and the sudden freedom of information and its amazingly convenient availability. Twenty-five years ago a farmer could research every tractor available on the market, but it would take him months, and perhaps years to do so. He would be sending countless letters requesting product catalogs or making long-distance phone calls seeking out the same. In fact, by the time he collected all of the materials he needed, half of the companies would have new products up for sale. For better or worse, the companies manufacturing the products were the ultimate gatekeepers on how information was distributed to potential customers. Consumers had word of mouth and sales pitches to rely on, comparison guides and message boards were still light years away.

That landscape has seen a complete reversal in the past 20 years. How much of the purchasing process is done online, with many consumers trusting their own research more than any salesperson interaction.

Consider:

92% of buyers start their process with an online search for information.

53% of buyers find that going online and conducting their own research is superior to interacting with a salesperson.

75% of buyers depend on social networks to learn about choosing the right vendor.

90% of buyers won't take a cold call from a salesperson.

Let's take a closer look at the staggering changes in the world of sales that those four prior statements imply.

92% of buyers start their process online: That immediately takes salespeople out of one of the most valuable parts of the sales process - initially guiding the customer toward a product the company thinks best solves their problem while likely also getting the company the best return on investment.

53% of buyers think their own online research is better than talking to a salesperson: Just like that, more than one-half of your potential target audience has declared they would rather go the road alone to talk to a person who is by all accounts an expert in the field. This does not just diminish a salesperson's role in the process, it puts their entire livelihood in jeopardy.

75% of buyers depend on social networks to learn about choosing the right vendor: Another form of cutting out the middleman is bringing the updated version of word-of-mouth advertising to the 21st century. It's another sign of the changing face of trust in the current crop of consumers. They'll listen to acquaintances and people they barely know faster than salespeople who might know everything about a product. Social media and message boards are the real litmus test for many because very few people post reviews on a product without a strong opinion. These reviews and recommendations are also polarized to the extreme positive and extreme negative, with little middle ground. That can be great or terrible for a company and its products, but is just another way that sales departments' roles are diminished evolving audiences.

90% of buyers won't take a cold call from a salesperson: Caller ID might have laid the first log on this bonfire, but the Internet set it ablaze. Despite the fact that we buy things nearly everyday, knowing that the person on the other end of a phone call has designs solely to sell us something has become something repugnant to a large portion of the population. Consumers want to be valued and tailored to, not have their phone numbers spit out of some giant computer somewhere as a likely candidate to buy something at random.

These stats and others like them are proof positive that traditional sales methods have become antiquated in the modern business world. Casting a wide net through cold calls, traditional advertising, or simply waiting for the next customer to walk through the doors of the brick-and-mortar location are no longer good for return on investment (ROI) and don't do anything to promote relational marketing.

MBS is an innovative approach designed to help your sales and marketing teams work together to deliver the right message to the right person in the right place at the right time. It is a sales call wrapped in a customer experience with the purpose of not just turning a lead into a conversion, but in opening a two-way conversational dialogue that finds the pain points of that consumer and begins the process of establishing a relationship that will build trust, rapport, and turn the first-time customer into a lifetime customer. When you can craft the perfect message, you execute your business objectives better, give the customer a better experience, and turbo-charge your ROI.

If your background is strictly in sales, the idea of relational marketing might be a bit tough to grasp. The sale is no longer the objective. A customer relationship is. You could compare it to the process of lighting a fire while out in the middle of the night in the woods.

The salesman is not thinking about the process of carefully arranging sticks, moss, and dry leaves together to start that first bit of kindling wood aflame. All he can see is the end result, the blazing bonfire that can be seen from miles around. But a carefully constructed fire doesn't work like that. It requires time and attention to grow from the first lick of flame up into a manageable campfire that gives you warmth, cooks your food, and lights your way. A smartly-built customer relationship is formed the same way. Trust, respect, and concern for the person comes first. When they are ready to move forward with the purchase of products, you are ready to assist them gather knowledge and make an informed decision. Over time, the fire will burn brighter and hotter until it is a constant, just like a pleased customer will return for more purchases and additionally adopt your brand as part of their lives.

When you invoke the MBS strategy to align your sales and marketing strategies, you begin to build that long-term fire. Using the tools mentioned in the lead of this book, you start collecting data on your potential customers and combine that with the personal touch that is so often lacking in the over-hyped business world of today.

Consider the following as you imagine tailoring your marketing and sales strategies together to revolve around the customer:

What if you are able to personalize your marketing narrative to your potential customers?

What if your sales message reflected your marketing and soft skills as well as your relationship-building skills?

What if your marketing and sales strategies both rotated around your potential buyer?

If all three of those questions could be answered in the positive, not only would you likely make a new customer, but also establish a strong business relationship that would last longer than just that first deal.

The new age task of blending marketing and sales is a bit like watching a great athlete in motion. If you've watched any of the past few Olympics, no doubt you've marveled at Usain Bolt, the legendary Jamaican sprinter who has racked up eight gold medals over the course of three Olympic games and holds the world record in both the 100 meter dash and 200 meter dash. When we watch Bolt run, we're riveted by his performance. One of the tallest sprinters in modern history, his fluidity of movements and his ability to perform a series of well-practiced moves is phenomenal. In these moments, it's easy to turn to a friend or fellow fan and exclaim something like,"Wow! He makes it look so easy!" Of course, in reality, what Bolt is doing is extremely challenging. Years of training have led Bolt to becoming the dominant athlete he is. He is the perfect combination of talent, vision, and repetition. Not to mention the patience and commitment necessary to practice day after day in all sorts of weather conditions, on the days when he wanted to stay in bed or avoid the gym. You might not be able to outrun Bolt, but in today's business world, you have a similar task if you want to attract and retain customers.

When you follow the MBS framework, your integrated marketing and sales efforts will find new life and new success. As you proceed through this book, we'll explore all steps in greater detail. But first, here's an overview to get you warmed up for the adventure ahead.

Our first destination will be Brand Marketing and how to create a winning brand value proposition, also known as a BVP. To do this, we'll ask questions geared to set our business apart from the rest. Questions such as what makes your brand special? If customers and prospects could know one thing about your brand, what would you want it to be? Why do you think that customers should pick your company instead of the competition?

From there, we'll dig into developing and using buyer personas. This is an area where technology can really benefit us and turn guesswork into analytical truths. If you want buyers to get to know your brand, you better know your buyers first. The biggest things you have to understand include what their needs are and what are their pain points? In other words, what is the reason they're out shopping around for your product and service in the first place, and what can you do to solve their problems?

Third is where marketing really has to dig in and expand its reach. It's time to use storytelling about your brand. It's time to put your heads together for some major collaboration and create engaging content that can create a story to delight the customer. Make it meaningful, memorable, and persuasive.

This is the time to dazzle your customers so they won't easily forget your brand.

Fourth, we'll make sure that storytelling success is not just a one time thing by developing a customer experience management strategy. This isn't just about making sales, this is about adopting a customer into your brand culture. It will require an omnichannel experience that keeps the customer focused on your brand no matter where they travel and let you take an inside look at how customers really experience your brand. Do they know what your brand stands for, what you hope to accomplish, and what your goals for them are? Do they even remember you at all? It's time to find some answers and step up your game to take a closer look inward.

Fifth, it's time to put your sales team to work. Mastering sales today is a horse of a different color from even 20 years ago. Not only do you need to master both hard and soft selling skills, but you'll need to be able to integrate them into any situation with considerable speed and flexibility.

And finally, we'll talk alignment. Not about marketing and sales, but about the big-picture items, namely your business goals and your customers' needs. If they are extremely disparate, you're going to have trouble with alignment, but if the two are in sync with one another, it's possible to have very satisfied customers engaging with a brand they know and respect, which in turn is achieving its goals, both financially and in terms of engagement.

MARKETING IS REALLY JUST ABOUT SHARING YOUR PASSION.

Michael Hyatt

CHAPTER 2

BRAND MARKETING: CREATE A WINNING BRANDVALUE PROPOSITION (BVP)

One of the biggest downsides of all the revolutions in technology that have taken the business world over the past few years is that there's no all encompassing user's manual for them. Corporations and organizations are scooping up software after software that look like they might make good sense to use in their system processes, but the actual planning is getting left to the side. There's an old saying that tells us that if you don't know where you're going, well, any road will take you there.

Far too many businesses are emulating that saying when it comes to marketing their products and services. They don't understand how to combine the various aspects of social media, Big Data, advanced analytics, and Artificial Intelligence together to develop a cohesive, integrated marketing communication strategy. And if you can't figure out how to get your message across, how can you possibly know if it's successful or not?

Where to begin this long, twisted journey through unknown territory? At the easiest place to do just that; The beginning. Before we go plotting out our brand strategy, we have to know what we have, what we're lacking, what we can rely on, and what can be a risk to the whole operation. For that, we need to analyze our brand's Strengths, Weaknesses, Opportunities, and Threats. Together, they form SWOT analysis.

For the rest of this book, we'll be using one overarching example of a company with a specific product so that we may refer back to it time and again and keep a steady picture in your mind's eye, so that you can ultimately analyze the entire module for your own company.

Our business example will be a startup organic dog food company called PawTastic Pup Treats. The business is based in San Diego, California, and wants to take a bite out of the local market before moving on to compete for shares of the state and national organic dog food markets.

When you begin a SWOT analysis, always try to hit the positives first. This will give you a good starting point and allow you to view your company holistically and objectively.

STRENGHTS — WEAKNESSES

THREATS — OPPORTUNITIES

STRENGTHS

What is your company good at? It's remarkable how many firms draw a blank when this question is asked of them. It's almost like they went into business just to make money, not solve a problem, address an issue, or make the world a better place. If you need some examples before diving in on your own brand, take a look around at some of the signature brands that dominate not just your country, but the entire world. Let's take Starbucks as an example. Whether you're in London, Capetown or New York City, if you order a venti mocha frappuccino with no whipped cream, you're going to get the exact same drink, although the price difference might shock you. That's largely due to the fact that Starbucks is outstanding at recreating the same high-end experience at any store in the entire world. The pastries will have pretty much the same variety, the baristas will be friendly and polite, the house music will stay the same, and the straws will be green.

Shift gears a minute and consider Disney, especially if you've been to one of its myriad theme parks and resorts spread across the world. No matter where you are, Disney is committed to delivering amazing family experiences. From the parks themselves to the associate restaurants, hotels, and attractions, Disney's staff members are always striving to make your experience magical, particularly when your children are along for the ride. From random interactions with costumed characters to extra passes to some of the parks' favorite rides, Disney scores through the roof when it comes to customer experience, which explains why some 70% of their customers are repeat customers.

For our example - PawTastic Pup Treats - we'll hit on some high notes that make the brand stand out. For starters, it's made of 100% organic ingredients; no fillers or artificial flavors or colors here! That is a great way to get noticed early in the game, especially in health-crazed Southern California. Another strength is our commitment to donating part of our profits to animal rescue shelters throughout the area in an effort to ramp up pet adoptions and curb the putting down process of animals in shelters. Our third strength that we want the public to be aware of is our playful side. Our spokesdog won a nation-wide contest to be the pup who represents our brand for the first year of our experience. We want customers to get in on the action too by submitting photos of their dogs to our website. The winner takes over as our new spokesdog and gets his or her photo put on the box. He or she also gets a year's supply of PawTastic Pup Treats.

Especially if you're just starting your business, this can be a tough nut to crack. If you don't know, you can poll existing customers or ask your employees. Don't be afraid to be confident in your abilities here. If you don't know off the top of your head, do some self-analysis. What are your capabilities? Study your processes and determine where your resources lie.

WEAKNESSES

Next, it's time to detail your weaknesses and there's no point in bending the truth here, you will only hurt yourself. Ignoring them or reshaping them will only burn you down the road, possibly fatally. Knowing your biggest weaknesses allows you to point them out and get them addressed before a customer notices them, or worse, a competitor who could exploit them. But turning a weakness into a strength can not only shore up holes in your business plan, it can also be a defining moment that drives future success. Consider the LEGO brand. For decades, the chief complaint was that the company did not support its fervent fan bases, and did not introduce popular culture figures into its toy lines. Eventually, they followed the hint and LEGOs are arguably more popular than ever, having formed partnerships with enormous pop culture icons like the Star Wars, Harry Potter, and Jurassic Park film series along with DC comics. Not just toys any longer, LEGO has branched out into theme parks, four successful movies, a number of video games, and television series.

Over at PawTastic Pup Treats, our biggest weakness is our delivery process. We keep running into troubles at the warehouse where we pull stock too quickly, it doesn't sell, and then the expiry date hits and we're out that money for good. We're also not getting any traction outside of a very small area in San Diego. How do we appeal to dog owners outside of a certain affluent neighborhood where two stores have agreed to stock our product?

OPPORTUNITIES

This is where you need to start wearing your visionary hat and be able to move beyond simply selling your products and collecting revenue. Opportunities are everywhere, but it's up to you to determine which ones can benefit you the most, and which ones are better left on the wayside. Opportunities can come through partnerships, but they also come when there is any sort of social, technological, or industry change. A great example is Netflix. Its initial business model was selling DVDs and renting them through a mail service. This was a successful model for a few years as DVDs were the main media interface for movie fans. But as Internet speeds picked up, the cloud technology emerged, and streaming became a thing, Netflix was the first to grasp that it could replace the antiquated 'snail-mail' approach to reaching customers and made renting a movie quite literally as easy as pushing a button. It is not hyperbole to consider this achievement the equivalent of catching lightning in a bottle by seeing an opportunity and taking advantage of it. In a single stroke of action, Netflix wiped out all of the costs associated with mailing DVDs out to customers and having to pay for them to be mailed back; it cut customers' wait times on watching movies down from a few days to one second; and it didn't even have to build its own technology stack to house the new delivery method, it simply piggybacked off of existing technology being used by cable companies.

Seeing opportunities requires that you escape the 'box' that your own business exists in and become an expert of the industry and a master of micro- and macroeconomics. This could mean emulating other companies that have achieved success in areas that you struggle. It could mean implementing new software to speed up your processes or cut down on your errors. It could mean staff training to shore up data leakages or partnering with a bigger brand on some sort of mutual exchange to push both products to more of their targeted audience.

Being based in Southern California, PawTastic Pup Treats has the advantage of a local celebrity not only buying our brand but also endorsing it on Twitter. A few direct messages later and we've worked out a mutually beneficial deal to supply the celebrity with free treats in exchange for a certain number of social media plugs per month directed at the celebrity's Twitter and Instagram followers. Since our treats are a shade on the expensive side, tapping into the celebrity's social circles is a great way to penetrate our target audience without sending a single dime in marketing costs.

THREATS

Threats are perhaps the most important of the four-prong SWOT analysis. While weaknesses might damage your business in the long run, threats are no-doubters. Just as you should be an industry and economic expert to seek out and recognize opportunities for your business, you should be the same way to realize the presence of development of threats that could be the undoing of your company. Threats take your strengths and use them against you. Being able to avoid threats by being flexible, transparent, or by pivoting your business model if necessary, are essential to avoid them.

The biggest eyesore example of a company not realizing the threats against it can be awarded to the Kodak camera and film company. What happened at Kodak's labs in 1975 was satire in its highest state. Mark Twain would have loved it. Kurt Vonnegut was likely upset he didn't think of the idea first. Steve Sasson, a 24-year-old engineer working for Kodak's R&D department, invented the world's first digital camera, and by doing so, also invented digital photography. His first camera was a cumbersome thing, requiring nearly a minute to actually display its device, and that in black and white. The first digital camera was patented three years later, at which time Kodak told Sasson he was forbidden from telling anyone outside of Kodak about what he had invented.

The reason? Kodak was the market dominator at that point in history. According to the Economist, Kodak sold 85% of all cameras in the US in 1976. Personal photography needed four things at the time: cameras, film, chemicals, and paper to print the pictures on, and Kodak was the market leader in all four things.

In 1989, Sasson and colleague Robert Hills created the first modern SLR camera which had a 1.2 megapixel sensor and memory cards, much like the ones used today. Kodak's reaction was the same as it had been 14 years earlier. Patent the thing and put it in a closet somewhere.

The company made billions off that patent, but steadfastly refused to move away from its tried-and-true model of printed pictures.

The patent expired in 2007 giving other companies free use of it without paying royalties to Kodak. The former film giant tried to make the switch to digital and failed, declaring bankruptcy in 2012.

During the height of its empire, Kodak's advertising pitch was that "Kodak Moment" - the perfect picture of something special. Looking back on the company's steadfast refusal to abandon its flawed value proposition gives us a new definition of the Kodak Moment - the instant when you turned away from evolving technology, what the market needed, and changing times, and failed to realize a huge threat staring you right in the face. Turning a blind eye to the future and believing your business will endure as it always has crippled Kodak. How can you keep the same thing from happening to your business?

Another great example is what happened to Blackberry, the precursor to the modern smartphone. The first product to carry the name Blackberry was a two-way email pager released in 1999 in Germany. It was a smash hit with customers by 2002 because it resembled a tiny computer that could fit in the palm of your hand with a working keyboard and the ability to act as a telephone, email reader, text messenger, Internet fax machine, Web browser, and more. Its population erupted and it was the dominant leader in handhelds for most of the rest of the decade, easily outpacing PalmPilot.

As technology grew, the shift to touch screens that required finger swipes instead of buttons pushed became obvious, but BlackBerry ignored it, choosing to focus on its tried and true model and the millions of customers it already had, apparently not thinking about the billions of customers in the world who had no smartphone but were looking to enter the market.

The touch screen delivered one uppercut, and the fact that the screen size on the nebulous iPhones and Android devices was dramatically larger as a result, was the knockout punch. In the second quarter of 2013, Blackberry had still sold 6.8 million handsets, but half a year later, it cut 40% of its operating staff, some 4,500 positions, and dropped its product line from six models down to four. In June of 2008, the company's stock had peaked at $149.90/share. In September 2013, the entire company was sold for $9/share, less than 6% of its highwater mark.

Threats can come from just about anywhere, which is why your SWOT is more of a snapshot in time than a put-it-in-concrete device. Threats can be external or internal. Have your employees signed non-compete clauses in their contracts? If not, what's to stop one of them from taking your idea, tweaking it, and going into business for themselves? Is your company a small business providing a similar service or product to a larger firm? If so, and if the larger company sees your business as a threat, it can focus its efforts on undercutting you and driving you out of business. Being aware of threats is not enough, you have to have contingency plans to deal with them if they become realistic threats. This can mean anything from securing your copyrights to getting employees to sign more legally binding papers about their commitment to your company to finding opportunities that can guarantee the company's continued stability.

In our PawTastic Pup Treats example, the biggest threat to our success is the existence of big chains like Petsmart who have a dozen organic dog treats on their shelves not to mention a dozen more non-organic treats that pull away even more of our potential customers. They can run circles around us in advertising and being able to buy or produce treats in bulk allows them to beat us with a lower price as well. Battling these threats can only be achieved by getting our product in front of customers in other ways, such as by partnering with local veterinarians to display them in their offices, by having a terrific social media strategy to really communicate with our customers and incorporate their ideas into our structure, and to simply make a better-tasting, better-for-your dog product. The big chain can undercharge us if they like, but if we can offer a product that is better for your dog and better-tasting too, we're right back in the fight.

When your SWOT analysis is complete, the next big question to ask is, where do we want to go as a company? The answer is not "the bank" or "a tropical island in the South Pacific." That's the answer to what you want out of your company when you decide to hang it up. Ask yourself instead, what do you want the company to look like in 5, 10, or 20 years? If you're operating out of your garage right now, do you still want to be there in 2030? If not, where should you be, how many employees do you want? How broad should the reach of your product or service be?

What kind of brand can you create to get you to those numbers and places? Your brand value proposition (BVP) must reflect not only what you do, but what you believe as a company.

And here's the trick that will separate you from the competition: Don't focus on what you sell. That's not the most important thing. Focus on the solution you offer. Consider the Subway restaurant brand. It started in 1965 and now has more than 42,000 restaurants worldwide, more even than McDonald's. Between 1998-2011, the brand tripled in size thanks in large part to its adoption of Jared Fogle as a national spokesman after reports that he had lost more than 200 pounds by eating at Subway frequently. The ad campaign allowed Subway to position itself as being a healthy alternative to fast-food restaurants like McDonald's, Burger King, Jack in the Box, etc. Subway now was the solution to the problem so many people identified with: Where can I get a quick meal that isn't made of hamburgers, French fries, and other fatty foods?

Subway captured the answer to that question and rode it literally to the top of the food chain, at a time when many people were beginning to eat much more healthy as more and more evidence came out about how bad things like cholesterol and saturated fat were for the body. You don't have to save the world, cure cancer, or build a better mousetrap for your product to succeed. What you do need is to identify a problem that your customers have and offer them a solution.

In our example, PawTastic Pup Treats isn't doing anything that a dozen other brands in the market haven't tried before - an all-natural dog treat that doesn't expose your four-legged friend to artificial flavors, colors, and ingredients. But what we do have in our corner is taste. Most dogs will eat just about anything digestible, but there are always finicky ones in the pack. We have conducted research on the 75 most popular breeds of dog in the US and found that all 75 love our unique combination of ingredients. We believe PawTastic Pup Treats is the best-tasting organic dog treat on earth and even finicky eaters will gobble it up like a T-bone steak. We've answered the question, what organic snack is out there that even the most finicky of dogs will dive right into. We add a second point that when dogs crunch on our PawTastic Pup Treats, it also helps strengthens and cleans their teeth. Now our BVP is augmented by the fact that PawTastic Pup Treats can reduce your dog's dental needs while also delivering a healthy, delicious snack.

Answering the question is just scratching the surface on your BVP. A strong BVP isn't just a one-line answer on why customers should use your product, it is an all-points bulletin that drives things including messaging, special offers, sponsorships, community events, even research and development. You don't want to flood your customers with too much information, but you do want enough of it on hand so that if potential costumers have questions, you are giving them the easy-to-reach resources to solve every single one of them. To refine our BVP along those lines, we cue it up to move through the following five-step process.

STEP ONE: SET PROJECT OBJECTIVES AND SCOPE

In layman's terms, objectives are what you wish to accomplish with your business. Scope is how much you're going to include - will this be at your initial store and last for six months? How many units of your business will it cover? Just marketing? Just sales? Social media? All three? Or will it be at every location you have and be the new normal? There are two big questions that you must answer going forward with objectives and scope:

What value do we deliver to our customers?

Why do our customers buy from us?

It's possible that those two questions have similar answers, but they definitely need to both be explored regardless. Not only should these answers be reasonable, but they also need to be actionable, and focus on your target personas (more on that later). Value can be physical, emotional, intrinsic or a combination of all three. If you sell lawnmower parts, your product carries physical and intrinsic value to customers. Physical in that they are needed to fix a broken lawnmower, and intrinsic because your customers are the type of people who do their own lawn maintenance. If they can't get their mower fixed, they'll have to hire someone to do it for them, which will be a loss of additional money. If your store sells rare dolls and accessories for the American Girl line of collectibles, your product carries all three types of value. This knowledge can have a tremendous effect on how you market your goods and services, so you must have a clear view of that value.

The same is true about the reasons customers buy from you. You must conduct analytics and questionnaires to understand why they purchase the way they purchase items. Getting that user input is mission critical to continuing to do what you do well and finding ways to turn weaknesses into strengths moving forward. It might be your great customer service or your ability to keep the right parts in stock or the fact that you'll match any price in town if they bring in an ad showing a lower offering. Hopefully you can gain some real insight into how customers feel about what you produce and what it does for them. When you hear phrases like "It's the best set of golf clubs under $400" or "It's our go-to dessert place on date nights," that's the kind of power you can really harness and turn into something really actionable.

In regards to scope, we want a balanced design that lets all facets of your business get involved in driving the BVP forward: Marketing, traditional media, earned media, and things like social employee advocacy. Get your staff brainstorming and excited about what the company is about and what you're going to do going forward. Take suggestions from all angles as you build your strategy; leave no stone unturned.

At PawTastic Pup Treats, we deliver the best-tasting organic dog treats in town, and one that can help your dog's teeth be more healthy, reducing the amount of money you need to spend on getting your canine's teeth cleaned at the vet. When we poll our existing customers, they praise our innovation, they love the fresh factor of the treats, and they enjoy the opportunities to engage with us on social media and through contests.

STEP TWO: DEFINE YOUR POSSIBLE BVPS

This is your first real foray into the BVP experience, and wisely, you're not having to just choose one answer and stick with it. This is a phasing-in process where you're seeking to see which ideas stick and which still need refinement. Don't be afraid to throw ideas up against the wall at this point. Even things that are initially rejected might contain the kernel of ultimate truth that you need. Get a white board or several white boards and just start writing down ideas about what makes your company unique. Give a piece of paper to every employee you have and encourage them to do the same; sometimes the most obvious answer eludes you if you are too close to the project, just like authors who can't see the typo in the first sentence of the first chapter because they've gotten too close to the book to see it properly. Incentivize the project by offering a salary bonus to the person who delivers the best version of the possible BVP.

Look for inspiration around you, including with other companies. You're obviously not going to copy anyone else's work, but that doesn't mean they can't serve as points of inspiration. For instance, Walmart's BVP is that they offer the lowest prices around. You can't say the same thing, but say you sell bird seed for 30% less than the average pet store. You can easily call yourself the most inexpensive supplier of bird seed without infringing on Walmart or bending the truth in the slightest. Your BVP does not have to be about numbers, dollars, or statistics, although that's a commonplace idea for many. Your BVP can also be functional or emotional, as long as your customers can connect to them. Using functionality is BVP in its most simple form. If your company sells replacement parts for copy machines, your BVP could simply be: We fix copiers. It's short and to the point, no bells and whistles, and nothing that suggest you're trying to be anything more than what you are. The type of customers that are simply looking to have their copy machines repaired as quickly and painlessly as possible. They don't need an emotional connection, just results.

The opposite is true when you're rolling with an emotional BVP. When Steve Jobs was the face of Apple, you never had to be tech savvy or even speak English to find his new-product talks to be must-see entertainment. Jobs transcended language and understanding of "how stuff works" to bring each new

Apple innovation to the masses. Whether it was that first Macintosh computer that told us all "Hello", the first iPod, iPad, or that first glorious iPhone, when we saw it, we knew it was cool, and we knew we had to have one - price and availability be damned. Your customers' wants and needs are pivotal to include at this stage. If your target audience is big into conservatism, the fact that your company uses renewable energy to power its computer processors is huge. If your customers are more interested in results than a song-and-dance sales pitch, the fact that you don't use customer service reps, just knowledgeable employees can be a big difference maker.

At PawTastic Pup Treats, we hone in on three possible BVPs: That our pup treats are the best tasting in the business; that we are recommended by more San Diego vet offices than another other brand in the area; and that we never use artificial colors, flavors, or preservatives in our snacks. Input from our valued customers lets us know that they love the truly organic nature of our brand, that their pets routinely beg for more PawTastic Pup Treats, and that they like how the makeup of the treats helps clean dogs' teeth, meaning less time and money spent at the vet for cleanings.

STEP THREE: REFINE YOUR BVP

Now that you've got a few finalists, start to drill down on them and see which ones really hold up under fire. A lot of this will include talking to customers and analyzing how they are interacting with your brand across different channels, including traditional advertising, social media, and response to planned customer interaction events. What about your brand resonates the most with your consumers? If they have used your competitor's brand, or even just know about it, what about that brand resonates the most with them? We call this qualitative analysis and it's the lynch pin on how you'll move forward. Really monitor things like social channels and review websites such as Google and Yelp! These are the atmospheres where you're going to get the unfiltered scoop on what is really being said about your product. Prepare yourself for the worst and the best and let this be a learning experience. Some people will just be on this forum to vent, but there's always a kernel of truth in every bad review. Find the things that are attracting people to your brand and build on them.

At PawTastic Pup Treats, we offer customers a free bag of kibble in exchange for submitting an online questionnaire giving their honest opinion on our brand and the way we do business. We know their opinions in this forum might be slightly skewed to the positive - after all, we just did give them a free bag of dog food, so we hedge our best by poring over Twitter, Facebook, and Instagram for any and all references to our products. When we do find a reference or a mention, we track it, and reach out to whomever first made the comment and pick their brains about how they see our brand.

STEP FOUR: DEVELOP MESSAGING ARCHITECTURE FOR KEY SEGMENTS

No matter how good your message is, the biggest thing that can make or break your success, it's time to get your message out, but you need to do so carefully so you're not wasting time, effort, or money, you need to blend together what your customers want, what the standards of your industry require, what your company's budget is, and what forms of messaging are available to your company.

A lot of research must be done at this stage on how your audience likes to be connected with. If you're selling hearing aids and your main target audience is men and women over the age of 65, a slick ad campaign centered around Twitter and Instagram is not going to be the way to go. Similarly, if you have a new energy drink that helps rehydrate the body after a long night of clubbing, you're not going to advertise in community newspapers in the suburbs. Your messaging architecture is the foundation of what will become the customer experience, an absolutely vital part of the way you communicate with your customers and guide them to learn more about your company and your products, eventually leading to a purchase and hopefully the start of a long-term relationship. The missing factor for a lot of companies at this point is good old-fashioned creativity - marketing and sales professionals thinking beyond the standards of their professions and finding a really unique way to guide their messaging to target audiences. This is not the time to play it safe and take it slow. Roll the dice and see what sort of chemistry you can develop with your audience that can make you stand out in the crowd. At PawTastic Pup Treats, this is where we can really differentiate from the rest of our field, especially those big chains that carry similar products, but also carry a host of items for other animals and can't really focus in on the same target audience we can. We pursue people who give social media accounts to their dog and ask them for a like (or a woof). We engage with local vet offices to promote our product with some combination taste testing and vaccines or nail trims or free bath events to get the public out to see us and meet us, and give them a chance to really identify with our brand and the faces behind it. Let them see how much we love dogs and how much we would love to get our customers' input into how to keep putting out best foot forward to engage with the public as much as possible on what the No. 1 goals for pet owners and their pets are when it comes to our treats. We can even consider the customer's journey to be the equivalent to a dog's journey around the house or the yard to find a tasty treat and include the dog on the journey the customer takes through the sales funnel.

STEP FIVE: DETERMINE YOUR EXPECTED OUTCOME

That title might sound a little pie in the sky, but remember, it's your expected outcome not your desired outcome. Unless you've come up with some otherworldly device that can reverse time or make money appear out of thin air, there's going to be a ton of competition in whatever industry you intend to plant your stakes in. And with digital technology and the ease of creating online businesses, the level of competition has never been greater. Industries aren't just crowded with similar businesses, they are stuffed to the gills. If you have a great original idea, don't hold your breath - someone will be along in no time to replicate it and start trying to undercut the profits that you have started earning. It's just the nature of the beast, and the real-time connectivity that we all hold as such a blessing can also be a curse as any success story gets found out quickly, exposed to the rest of the world, and quickly copied.

Famed marketing guru Seth Godin turned the world on its ear when he published his book "Purple Cow: Transform Your Business by Being Remarkable". The idea is a simple one: if you want your business/product/service to stand out in a crowd, you have to be something totally unique that enables you to stand apart from the crowd so that the audience is focusing on you alone. There are a number of different ways to cultivate that purple cow, any one of which can be the winning solution for your product. It might be that you differentiate your customers and find the groups that are the most likely to be social media influencers or the ones that are the most profitable and focus on them. Or find an underserved niche to target and go to dominate. Exploring your limits is another purple cow option to consider. If you're the fastest already, how could you get any faster? Even if you're comparing you against yourself, you can always find some way to improve and share that improvement. You can also find things that are no longer or never have been done in your industry and start practicing them. Have your CEO (maybe it's you) hand-deliver products every week to show you're still connected to the people.

The managing team at PawTastic Pup Treats wanted to make dogs the central piece of our marketing pitch, so every commercial we've run on television so far has starred nothing but pooches so far, with a few human voice overs to break down the action. It's not costing an arm and a leg, and it probably gets more attention from other dogs and the family's kids than any other commercial on TV. Determining your expected outcome simply means gathering all the information you can and guessing what the future will offer. We aren't looking for long-term prognostication down to the dime, but rather what the results of this particular endeavor will look like. Use past indicators and current performance variables to see what your current outcome will be. Compare the answers with your predictions to see how accurate you have become.

When you've walked through these five steps, you'll likely have a much clearer look at what your brand is and what it's capable of. Being able to see yourself in the eyes of your customers is even more valuable because that perception determines how you look in the eyes of a consumer. Your BVP is the ultimate confidence-building guide to what makes your product special and why consumers should buy it from you instead of a similar product from another company. Once you've staked your claim, you can defend it by highlighting your brand's quality, innovation, and value.

Steps for creating a winning BVP:

SWOT

SET PROJECT OBJECTIVES

DEFINE YOUR POSSIBLE BVPS

REFINE YOUR BVP

DEVELOP MESSAGING ARCHITECTURE FOR KEY SEGMENTS

DETERMINE YOUR EXPECTED OUTCOME

AMAZING THINGS WILL HAPPEN WHEN YOU LISTEN TO THE CONSUMER.

Jonathan Midenhall

CHAPTER 3

HOW TO DEVELOP AND USE BUYER PERSONA

When it comes right down to buyer personas for your business, there's nobody more important than the Who.

No, not legendary British rockers Pete Townshend and Roger Daltrey, we're talking about the everyday consumers like you and me who are the target audiences for a million different businesses out there.

Why do buyer personas matter so much? Well, in a nutshell, it's because knowing who you are selling your product or service to, makes it a lot easier to sell it to them. That might not sound like the greatest philosophy in the world, but it's so often the simplest truth that winning brands turn into their biggest triumphs. Cultivating buyer personas is a great job for the powerful digital business tools we've spoken about at length in this book. They are excellent for collecting the bits of data about consumers that allow us to analyze what they like to buy, when they like to buy it, how much they are willing to spend on it, and a whole lot of other different factors that coalesce into the image of the very person we're striving to sell our wares too.

There's no end to the amount of demographic and market data that you can collect, research, and analyze thanks to digital technology. But the fact of the matter remains that you are not selling your product to a bunch of data points, you are selling it to flesh-and-blood people who have thoughts, emotions, doubt, fears, interests, and dreams. Building the personas of such people can be difficult, but taking this process seriously and working to make them as realistic as possible not only allows you to develop a winning message strategy that humanizes all your research, but also allows you to empathize with your customers' pain points and do a better job of guiding them along toward a resolution.

The overarching goal of buyer personas is to provide an authentic, impactful customer experience. To develop that, you need an audience to write for. The personas you construct are not real people, merely characteristics of what the ideal buyer looks like for your product or service being offered. Gathering these characteristics and building the persona - usually more than one - gives your marketing team valuable resources to get inside the buyers' minds and think how they think. This move is also at the heart of the MBS strategy we referred to in the beginning of this book. The customer is the central piece of intelligence in your strategy. The more you can know about that centerpiece of your strategy, the better you can expect your business to do.

Where most businesses fail or simply fall short on vision is when it comes to the number of personas they generate. It's not that you need 50 buyer personas, but you do need to create personas for people who aren't the actual buyers. What does that mean? Let's think about it with an example beyond our PawTastic Pup Treats. When it's time for a family of four to purchase a new car to replace the one that's on its last legs - or wheels as the case can be, there's a general buzz of excitement permeating the household. Although taking on a new car payment is never a fun situation, all eligible parties will be appealing to the ultimate decision-maker (and loan signer) on what makes, models, and colors they want to see their new ride possess. Stick shift or automatic? Racy red or thoughtful green? Leather seats? New or used? Lease or own?

Whether it's the husband or wife ultimately putting their name on the loan, they become the primary buyer persona for that car. But the rest of the family can be thought of secondary buyer personas because they all influence the purchase decisions, building empathy for their needs, their concerns, and their pain points with the ultimate buyer.

We need to create personas not only for the potential buyers but also for those that are around and can influence the purchase decision, building empathy for their needs, their concerns and pain points.

A more modern example would be a company that creates and sells educational software apps to be used in the classroom. In very few cases would the end-users of this product, teachers and students, be making the final decision on whether or not to invest in the app. The software development company knows that it's really selling to a technology person who is probably a mid-to-upper level executive in a school district's hierarchy. But they are also selling the product to the school board members who will ultimately approve or deny the funding for it. On an even more intimate level, they are selling it to the teachers who have clamored for apps that do more of a certain something, and selling it to the students who will be using it day in and day out and who will ultimately approve or disapprove of the app. Their voices will be heard loudest and longest either singing its praises or dragging it through the mud. Therefore, secondary buying personas must be built to take into all of these important moving pieces of the larger decision.

But enough talking about the process, let's dig into it and use our endearing dog treat example to see how it is done.

Here's how to get started building buyer personas, by gathering reliable buyer data first.

As has been mentioned multiple times throughout this book, collecting data is no longer a problem for any company with even the most basic of digital tools. These trackers can determine what customers are doing when they open your emails, examine your social media posts, visit your website, etc. The buyer data you're gathering can come from many different sources and includes, but is not limited to such categories as:

Demographics

Psychographics

Geography

Purchase behaviors

Social media behavior

Independent observation

Social media such as LinkedIn, Facebook, and Instagram, and review websites like Yelp or TripAdvisor or Google are fantastic for building buyer personas in particular because they contain unfiltered opinions of what buyers are really thinking about what you're selling.

When you get your data collected, sifted, and analyzed, you can start building the buyer personas. This will take extra demographic research into a "day in the life" of the people whose information you are using to construct the persona. You can foment this research by asking yourself key thought-provoking questions such as:

What is their demographic information?

What does a day in their life look like?

What are their buying habits?

What are their hopes, dreams, and aspirations?

What are their pain points? How do you help them solve them?

What do they value most? What are their goals?

Is your customer B2B or B2C?

What are their most common objections to your product/ service?

Who influences their buying decisions?

That is a long list of 'who' questions to begin the building process, but there's more to the persona than that. You also have to consider where a customer is in the buying process. Did they just hear about your product yesterday or have they just now decided to contact you after months of exhaustive research?

Where is almost important as who. If the customer you're communicating with is ready to pull the trigger on buying your product after researching it independently for two weeks, they're going to be turned off when your first round of communication is giving the basics on a product. Similarly, the consumer just doing their first round of Google searches on your product and stumbling across your website is unlikely to want to be pushed into a corner as you attempt to close a quick sale.

Where a consumer is in the customer journey can also turn into an unexpected pain point that your messaging must consider and attempt to rectify it. Let's take a look at another example to drive that point home.

Say your company is an online supplement supplier for athletes. After the negative attention brought forth by creatine, PEDS, and so on, business is booming as athletes are taking better care of their bodies and being careful about what they put in them to speed up recovery time and build muscle mass. The last two years have been a steady success and sales have risen slowly but consistently. But lately, things are going the wrong way. It's an oddity because your analytics show that there is no corresponding hit being taken on your website, if anything traffic is up. Launching an investigation, you use trackers to see where along the web process customers are getting bogged down. They're clicking a lot of links, reading a lot of product descriptions, putting items into their virtual carts, and then you see the problem.

It's digital cart abandonment, something that plagues every online retailer in the world at one time or another. Some experts have it hitting as high as 80% of all visitors who start a transactional process on a website. The fact that customers are leaving carts abandoned isn't that shocking, but you need to find out why and what you can do to lower that number. Brainstorming must follow, not just by you, but by as many brains as you can put on it, including anyone on your team that has knowledge of this part of the sales process.

Brainstorming commences and you have several possible causes:

A breakdown in the website progression that leads to an error on the customer's end or some sort of malfunction.

Competitors are offering to give them a better deal and customers are abandoning their carts when they can see the price you're offering and buying elsewhere.

Something in the fees, like taxes or shipping, is turning consumers off.

You've identified the problem and come up with a few potential reasons for it, now it's time to check the data. If you've opened those coveted two-way lines of communication, you can generally figure out where the downturn is coming through much more quickly. Are you encouraging regular customer feedback? Are you using trackers to see where customers are going after they leave your site and where they came from when they got there? Are they visiting sites of your competitors? When's the last time you visited competitor sites and went through their version of the buyers' experience to see how it is similar to yours? If nothing else, this is a great way to see how their sites differ from yours and what challenges / problems they might have that you can use to your advantage.

Taking that deeper look into customer feedback allows you to come away with the insight that your brand is getting great reviews for overall quality, but lower rankings when it comes to price. That only adds to your confusion because having a lower price point than most of the competition has always been part of your BVP. Clearly, you are missing part of the information. You try social listening next since customer feedback is not always 100% reliable. Tracking your brand name on Twitter, Facebook, and Instagram lets you check out conversations being held about it, and when appropriate, the opportunity to ask questions about the things people are saying or the way they are feeling.

It can be really tempting to confront any social media user or blogger who is saying something negative about your brand should you find something to that effect, but that is not going to solve the problem. As you move through review websites, you at last find the culprit. While your brand is praised for its selection and its great discounts on some products, you are getting low marks for your return policy and your shipping arrangements, something that several of your competitors have taken advantage of and separated themselves from you accordingly. Your prices on individual items are the best in the business, but your price on shipping is lagging behind and causing the overall cost of ordering from your company to go up significantly. When customers see their total cost including shipping, they back off purchasing from you. Your system for returns and/or exchanges is also leaving something to be desired by your customers. Those two pain points are huge rifts in the way consumers view you. They know that free shipping by big brands is becoming more and more commonplace and are irked that your company is charging more for it. Having a return policy more complex than - here's a box, print this label, and we'll take care of the rest is also bothering your customers, who want to know their justification for returning a product is honored. Clearly the squeaky wheel is demanding some grease, but you have to be careful with how much oil you put on it. Your gut reaction might be to drop your shipping costs or remove them altogether, but that can make new pain points, such as your company going from a very specific profit per transaction to breaking even or even losing money.

In medicine, there's an old joke that sometimes the cure is worse than the disease. Think carefully about your solutions and be sure to test them for unexpected consequences before rolling them out to your customers.

MARKETING

MARKETING IS NO LONGER ABOUT THE STUFF YOU MAKE, BUT ABOUT THE STORIES YOU TELL.

Seth Godin

CHAPTER 4

BRAND STORYTELLING TO CREATE ENGAGING CONTENT

You've got your buyer persona lined up, refined your Business Value Proposition and locked in on your SWOT. Now it's time to bring your value proposition to life. That doesn't mean decorating your website with flashy lights and fancy videos, nor does it mean you need to hire a celebrity to stand in front of the teleprompter and extol the virtues of your product.

No, what you want and what your audience will crave, is a story.

That's right, much like the preschooler we all once were, the audience is wanting to hear the story behind how your product came to be and why they should buy it.

According to research from Stanford University, stories are up to 22 times more memorable than facts alone. Facts might look good in the quarterly report but stories have something that no report could ever duplicate: the ability to create meaningful emotions in those who read them.

Storytelling is no fly-by-night newcomer to the world of marketing and sales. It's one of the oldest traditions in human history, predating writing by thousands of years. In the earliest of days, tribes of humans passed down their greatest stories, their mythology, and everything they knew about their families by storytelling. A storyteller in a village was highly revered, and whomever he chose to train as his replacement shared that honour.

Storytelling has been such a powerful part of human history that our brains have evolved to accept it and react to it. When we hear things about a delicious meal, our sensory cortex activates. If we're told a story about someone running for their lives, our motor cortex does likewise. When someone tells us about a perfume that smelled like strawberries or the wind howling during a rainstorm, we can sense it almost as strongly as if we were the ones to actually experience it.

The first time we experience a story, we form powerful bonds to it when it connects with us emotionally. Think about a favorite movie that you like and how well you can remember seeing it for the first time and what resonated with you.

One of the most-watched movies of all-time is George Lucas's 1977 sci-fi classic Star Wars, which has spawned 10 other feature films, including one released in December 2019 - more than 42 years after the original debuted. Some of the most iconic scenes in movie history dotted the film's landscape, including young Luke Skywalker gazing out at the horizon as he seeks adventure instead of his boring home life, defiant Princess Leia looking on in horror as her home planet is destroyed, and noble Obi-Wan Kenobi sacrificing himself to Darth Vader's lightsaber so that his young friends can escape. That kind of emotional connectors hang around with people for years and decades, not minutes and hours.

Thus, the question becomes, what's your story and what are you doing to tell it? Not only what the story is, but how you tell it, is absolutely essential when it comes to crafting the tale of your business product. This is your chance to captivate an audience, get them invested in what you are selling, and make them want to be a part of that success story.

That kind of behavior is what we call unlocking the emotional core of your brand. While all businesses certainly strive to turn a profit somewhere down the road, almost all of them have an underlying reason for going into business in the first place. Perhaps it's to take up the mantle of a family member who taught them how to cook, make woodworkings, ride horses, or build something. Or perhaps it's because the founder had a problem and invented a way to share it, now hoping to share it with as many people as possible. For others, it's a passion that has spurred them into creating their own business, meaning they can do what they love while they work - which is a goal that millions have, but are never able to fulfill. But you can, and you can share the knowledge of how you did it with your audience to make them buy into the same emotions that you have tapped when you started your business in the first place.

THE BIG FOUR QUESTIONS OF STORYTELLING

No two stories are alike, but crafting them using a step-by-step method is a great way to ensure success. As you build your story, fall back to these four questions to make sure you're covering all your bases and making your story as relevant, relatable, and remarkable as possible.

QUESTION ONE: WHY?

It's the big one, and quite frankly if you don't have an answer already, you need to do some serious thinking. Everything your business is about stems from the answer to this question. The "why?" answer is the reason why you are in business to begin with and the reason you're working all of those extra hours, nights, and weekends, not to mention straying away from traditional healthcare and retirement saving programs, skipping out on time with friends, etc. The answer to "Why" has to be one hundred percent original and relatable to convince others that it's true.

Remember our San Diego-based example of PawTastic Pup Treat? People will want to know why we started this business, what the impetus was for the high-quality organic ingredients, and so forth. We have a real story built in from our real lives. Several years ago, we took our favourite pooch to a dog show in the large metropolitan area special events center. There were all kinds of dog- and pet-related vendors on hand, and after conversing with one, we took a free dog treat with us to give to our dog later in the day. This dog treat was from a place that sold human desserts as well, and had cleverly made the dog treat into the shape of a hamburger with several blended colors to emulate the bun, cheese, meat, and various vegetable toppings as well.

That night, the dog got his treat, and within seconds we realized something was horribly wrong. He began shaking, crying, and had the canine equivalent of a seizure. After that, he refused to walk up the stairs to bed and we had to take him to the vet for a diagnosis. It was a seizure brought on by one of the dyes in the dog treat that made it so colourful. A chemical addition to keep the dog treats fresh and vibrant, it had instead sent our dog into a state of shock. He wasn't really back to himself for another 3-5 days.

After the incident, we decided that we needed to educate other dog owners on the dangers of pre-manufactured cookies and what to look for on the ingredients list before serving it to man's best friend. That approved to be a tough haul, so we took a different approach - selling our own brand of safe, delicious, organic dog treats to give people and their pets a safe alternative. Our love for our dog and all other creatures is the answer to Why?

This story obviously will be a powerful attractant for people with pets, especially those who have had a similar health scare. Whatever your story may be, make it the centerpiece of your brand so that you can transfer it to other customers and really showcase the value of your product or service. Don't let readers forget about the brand you have so carefully created.

QUESTION TWO: HOW?

So you've crafted the tale that got you from a dream in your head to a product, a store, a brand, a company. You've drawn in the customers and made them care about you and what you're offering. That's fantastic if you merely wanted a round of applause when you finished telling your tale, but that's just the first bite of the apple.

What you're looking for is to connect your customers to that story and give them a very specific, very genuine reason why they can benefit from your story and your product. The very essence of the storytelling procedure in the MBS process is transferring the value of your product from you to them.

What does your product do? What problem does it solve? Is it a tool? A luxury item? A necessity? A service? Does it make things easier for customers online? Does it keep them safe? Does it connect them better with their families? You need to be very specific here and tell the customer exactly what the product does and what problem it solves. Plenty of your audience might be smart enough to figure it out on their own, but you don't really want that. You want to tell the audience the "How" answer in your own voice with your own words. That way you are guiding them on the customer journey towards a decision-making process that provides them with precisely the information they need.

For our example business of PawTastic Pup Treats, we want the audience to know that they can keep their beloved pets safe from the harmful chemicals that infest plenty of artificial dog treats. These treats are made to last a long time in a container so they are injected full of chemicals and dyes that preserve them. Sure, they might last 3 months instead of 2 weeks, but it's at the cost of your dog consuming lots of artificial substances that add up an unhealthy cocktail. The level of dog owner we are chasing is one that is moderate-to-majorly involved in the dog's life. The person who buys 40-pound bags of bulk dog food from the wholesaler for the cheapest price possible is not in our target audience. The ones who buy higher-end dog food because they know its ingredients are healthy, not just filler, is who we are after.

Because these consumers value the importance of more healthy ingredients, they pay more for their dog food. That means they are willing to pay more for dog treats that they deem to be healthier and safer for their dogs as well. By conveying the idea that PawTastic Pup Treats are not only delicious, but also safe, healthy, and made from 100% organic materials, we are hooking the customer with a trio of value propositions that will have them interested to see if our product measures up to the smell test with both human and canine.

QUESTION THREE: WHAT?

If you've nailed down the 'How' and the 'Why', the 'What' speaks for itself. Just ask what niche do you serve? What is your vision of the future of that niche? The niche is an industry or more likely, a specialized sub-component of that industry. If you build smart sensors that monitor air conditioning and heating units for leaks and malfunctions, you could fit in any number of industries: the Internet of Things, sensors in general, HVAC tools, etc. You have to be able to really drill down and find that niche, because if you misfire and try to target the wrong audience, you'll be wasting your resources and getting very little Return on Investment (ROI). Take the time to research and see what sort of terms people are searching for when they turn to Google and other search engines looking for products like your own. This is one of the cases where imitation is the sincerest form of flattery; if you know what people are searching for when they find your competition, you'll know what they're thinking about and what industries they are coming from when they find your firm as well.

For our PawTastic Pup Treats, it would be easy to slap a dog food label on our product and be done with it, but that drastically devalues the product we're putting out there. As mentioned previously, our target audience isn't buying bulk rate generic dog food. We need to be very specific and target dog owners who are looking for organic alternatives to traditional treats and snacks. That niche might be small compared to some, but if you hit the nail on the head, you'll be racking up customers left and right.

That's your niche, and that's where you'll be working for a while, but what is your vision? To take your business across the city, across the state, or across the country? It doesn't have to include worldwide expansion to be a vision of the future, it could be expanding to complementary products, opening a brick-and-mortar store if you only dabble in online sales, or being part of a product line in a major department store.

At PawTastic Pup Treats, we might know that our market is somewhat limited to certain areas of California. Neighboring states like Arizona and Nevada aren't that well known for believing in the organic lifestyle the same way that a majority of Californians do. The vision could be doing most of our sales in the Southern California area both online and at a few brick-and-mortar locations in upper-class neighborhoods where dog owners are far more likely to engage with our brand. For consumers outside of Southern California, the products can be available via mail delivery.

QUESTION FOUR: WHO?

You've told the customer the reason that the product exists, why they should buy it, what niche your product fits in, and what the possible future might look like. Now there's one more thing left to sell: Yourself! That's right, you the owner, you the CEO, you the company. For some people, this is the single-most difficult part of the project because it is the most personal. As you grow along the lines of becoming an entrepreneur, you end up talking much more about your company or your brand or your product than you ever do about yourself. But consumers want to do like Toto in "The Wizard of Oz" and pull back the curtain to see the man or woman running the machine. If you use social media, this is a great opportunity to give a bit more insight into who you are and what makes you tick. Seeing a real person behind a brand is an enormous step of confidence when building a relationship between consumer and brand. One of the things that makes consumers suspicious when buying online is not knowing if the friendly website they've found is being run by the nice crew of people listed on the "About Us" page or by a single person in their spare room concocting images and names that make them look more reputable than they really are. So use this opportunity to let people see as much of the real you as you're comfortable with. For PawTastic Pup Treats, we'd definitely show a picture of the CEO or maybe every single employee with their own special pup. Tell the story in a series of blogs or an About Us page of whom our first dog or how long dogs have been a part of our life. Find new ways to show clients more about you so they'll identify as much as possible, and see your company as engaging people, not automated processes.

CREATING TWO-WAY CONVERSATIONS

When you're generating your own content, rather than relying on an overarching narrative from its manufacturer if you are a third-party vendor, you have much more control over the message itself, how it is delivered, and the quality. You can tailor your message specifically for your predetermined customer personae to match up with their pain points.

When you engage in social marketing - which can include social media, emails, text messages, blogs, and more - your goal is two-way interactions, not one-way monologues. Your content does not need to be preachy or written like a politician to win over a crowd. It needs to engage and make things as much about the audience as possible without losing track of the product you are selling. To achieve this, try out the 80/20 rule. That means that 80 percent of what you share needs to be about your brand's fans and customers, what makes them happy, markets information, insights, and how they relate to the brand. This will get a lot of dialogue coming from their part, and will give you lots of extra ideas for the future of how to engage with them. The last 20% should be about you and your business: Tell the audience what your new products are and what is possibly coming down the pipeline. Give them a taste of what the inside edition look of your company is without giving out any trade secrets.

A couple of examples of this sort of dialogue come from two of the biggest customer-oriented companies on the planet.

One is Mastercard, the credit card and financial services super power. It has previously used the marketing campaign of "Unlock priceless adventures" with your credit card. The information on the card is mostly muted, instead the focus of the campaign is about the Why, How, and What its cardholders can accomplish.

Another outstanding example is Coca-Cola, which has grown to be the world's largest non-technology company. Coca-Cola doesn't bother with breaking down the taste factor of any of its products, nor try to dazzle you with its market share (which is considerable). Instead, its campaigns are locked in on good feelings, friends, and shared memories. A popular recent radio ad for coke appears to be asking people what their favorite pizza is. A dozen responses ensue, all varied, except for the "and a Coke" tag at the end. Nowhere in there is Coca-Cola trying to sell you a product, it is merely perpetuating how good a Coke tastes alongside your favorite variety of pizza.

Now that you have seen some examples of how great two-way dialogue works, we can move on to the narrative you use for delivering your content. Voice, tone, and style are all huge decisions to make in the marketing and sales process. Coming at customers the wrong way will turn them off to whatever it is you're trying to sell, even if it's the perfect product for their pain point. Today's audiences are very specific in what they want from this conversation, namely information that is helpful, content that is easy to understand, and available on their own terms. What does that mean specifically? Let's take a closer look.

Helpful: Content must exist to fill a need or solve a problem for the consumer. If they feel it is just fluff designed to promote a product, they will depart rapidly.

Easy to understand: Most content writers aims to write at a level that is easily read by a 14-year-old with a standard education. Regardless of what industry your product is in, you need to write in language that does not exclude your intended audience. If a consumer feels like you're using terminology that they don't understand, it will be a big turnoff to them and make them feel that you are intentionally writing above their intelligence level. No one likes to feel stupid, and they definitely don't want to buy from a company that they believe is making them feel that way.

Availability: The way we buy things has changed in so many ways in the last quarter of a century that advertising and marketing professionals from two generations ago would scarcely recognize the current landscape. For a good 50 years, there were three ways to reach consumers: print, radio, or TV. Consumers were more geared towards taking what companies were offering them rather than deciding what they wanted for themselves and expecting customized orders. Companies were able to dictate the terms of how buyers learned about products, and things like annual catalogs sent through the mail were viewed as the Holy Grail as consumers eagerly anticipated them and then rushed to phone or mail in their order requests as soon as possible. The dawn of the digital age and the rise of the Internet and the subsequent creation of mobile communication devices (notably, smartphones, tablets, wearable tech), has completely upended that way of thinking. Consumers want and generally have total access to whatever information they want via the Internet, and can access it in any number of formats. Past the original big three, they can visit company/brand websites, read blogs and articles, join discussion groups, connect via social media, receive text messages, have experiences in enhanced or virtual reality, etc. Basically the consumer can receive your information in any form they wish, at any time.

The Big Four Questions of Storytelling:

CONTENT IS THE AUTOMATIC PARTICLE OF ALL DIGITAL MARKETING.

Rebecca Lieb

CHAPTER 5

CREATING YOUR CONTENT MARKETING STRATEGY

What your content marketing looks like and how you distribute it across the right channels for the right audience at the right time is the biggest obstacle to turning consumers into customers, and hopefully repeat customers.

Content marketing lies at the intersection of the content that brands like to publish and the content that consumers and prospects actually want.

Clearly we cannot just dump our content over all points of the Internet, cross our fingers, and hope that the right people stumble across it. We must plan a compelling content marketing strategy to ensure we are covering our bases and doing the very best we can to deliver the content that has the best chance of converting viewers into customers. There are five steps to follow when building a content strategy blueprint. While we are aware that different businesses have different motivations and sales strategies, and cover a wide pantheon of sizes, audiences, and products/services, this blueprint is scalable to your business, will reduce your marketing spend, drive revenue, and increase both visibility and brand recognition. The five steps follow here.

STEP ONE: CONDUCT A CONTENT AUDIT

Most people cringe when they hear the term 'audit', fearful that the government is coming to take a look at their taxes. But this kind of audit is the best medicine for discovering the current state of your content, including what is working well and what needs improvement. This is going to be a long process regardless if you've been generating content for two weeks or 10 years. You'll need to ask yourself some point-blank honest questions, and if you're the one who generated most of the content, you might consider asking someone else on your staff to do it, or hiring a third-party vendor who specializes in that sort of thing. Musts for this step include:

Does your supply of content map to your buying stages? Your buying stages are the points in the customer journey where you expect the customer to make key decisions on going forward in the buying process. They all don't revolve around making an actual purpose, but they are key spots where the consumer makes a choice. Your content needs to supply enough information to help the viewer make the choice to move forward and continue gaining knowledge.

Is the content relevant to your target persona? You might have hired the greatest content writer available to cook up some hip, 21st century humor for your company blog, but if your target audience is grandmothers over the age of 60, your content won't make any sort of impression (or a lick of sense) to your target audience. When you're performing your audit, you can fit content into three categories: Keep as it is, repurpose it, or move on without it. This can be frustrating if a lot of your established content falls into the second and third categories, but this strategy is devised to only keep 'the best of the best' while adding value to existing content that doesn't quite fit the bill in its current incarnation.

Is the content in sync with your brand value proposition (BVP)? Your BVP is the pillar that the rest of your strategy is built on, so it's a must that your content is delivering the same message to your audience. In some cases, this can be a simple adjustment of terminology in existing content, but if the message is too far gone, scrapping the piece is probably the best solution.

Is your content easily accessible on all of your audience's preferred touchpoints? A crucial question that we touched upon while talking about the plethora of ways an audience can engage with content. Let's think about it in terms of the old world of advertising - where print, radio, and TV were kings. If your business was to offer investment advice, it would make tremendous sense to advertise in the daily newspaper, knowing that most people who played the stock market back then were avid readers of the business section of the newspaper every morning while eating breakfast or on their commute to work. Knowing this, you wouldn't advertise your business during mid-day television programming because you know that your target audience isn't tuning in at that time. The same rationale is in effect in the present. Let's head back to Southern California and our old friends at PawTastic Pup Treats. We've established that their target audience are affluent pet owners who value things like organic ingredients and giving animals the best life possible. This type of person is very likely to be active on social media and Internet forums, where they can share opinions with others and make their voices heard to their followers. Using PawTastic Pup Treats' social media platforms to engage with these customers in a two-way conversation is the perfect way to deliver content to them. Writing articles and blogs, or posting videos that are easily shareable to social media is also a great way to reach them, convince them, and have them share your stuff to potentially convince others as well.

STEP TWO: REMEMBER YOUR BRAND VALUE PROPOSITION (BVP)

Remember your BVP? The most effective form of content links your BVP to the story of your brand. When you can establish that connection, you can forge a chain that is strong at both ends and lets each side strengthen the other. While content is ostensibly to promote your brand and your products, it must also specifically target your customers and their needs, in order to give them the sense that the biggest part of your product is how it serves them best. Answering the following three questions is a great way to ensure that what you are offering is what customers are looking for.

What value do we deliver to our customers? Value is a word that we really cannot overuse. In order to acquire our product or service, customers are taking some of their own earned money and giving it to us. They are not just buying a thing, they are buying its value. Content marketing is the means to establish that value with the customer to the point they are willing to exchange one for the other. If they are unsure that your product is worth their money, the chance of them buying it decreases rapidly. If they buy your value and it does not live up to the anticipated value, you will not retain them as a customer and have to start the process all over again with a new lead.

Why do customers buy from us? While their answers will likely vary in a survey, we want to give them one overriding answer as the reason they should buy our product. For a brand like BMW, luxury is the answer. Now that single word encompasses a lot of other adjectives, like "speed," "status," and "comfort," but BMW is one of the premiere luxury automotive companies in the world, and its advertising and other collateral messaging reflects that consistently. Contrast that to a brand like Walmart, the US base chain of mega-retailers that operates more than 10,000 stores spanning 27 countries. Walmart's success is based on its ability to sell a pantheon of products at the lowest prices on the market thanks to its ability to buy great volumes of merchandise at bulk-rate discounts, and pass the savings on to consumers. Walmart isn't going to dazzle its customers with phenomenal customer service or use celebrities to endorse its products. It stands by its commitment to the lowest prices, period.

Why should they care? This can be a tough question to even ask yourself, let alone answer it! Most entrepreneurs are so convinced that their product is the one to change the world that they sometimes forget that the world isn't desperately looking for the best new thing all the time. For every product, there's going to be a segment of the audience that is out looking for a product, finds yours, and buys it without much hesitation. This is an extreme majority of your audience. The rest are either passively interested or not interested at all, and need to be convinced that what you are offering is an essential for solving a problem or improving some facet of their lives. If your content cannot do that, there is zero motivation for them to trade their money for something they do not believe in. Put yourself in their shoes. Say you have a flower garden in your yard that does reasonably well. You suppose it might be nice to spruce it up with some different fertilizer, but it's not very high on your overall priority list. If you get an email for a new type of fertilizer that promises decent results and lists all sorts of statistics for oxygen penetration and solubility that you don't understand, nothing about that content is going to push the needle for you on trading your money for the fertilizer's value. However, if the email catches your eye with vibrant colors of a wide range of flowers that can be grown with this new fertilizer, along with the fact that they will last twice as long as other brands, and that a well-manicured yard can increase the value of your home up to 15% when you're ready to sell, suddenly you're wanting to know more about it. It's all about finding the proper triggers to drive consumers towards becoming customers.

STEP THREE: TARGET BUYER PERSONAS AND YOUR STORY

The buyer personas you created earlier are a powerful tool that can be used again and again to hone several parts of your business to cater exclusively to your target audience. After all, the better you know your buyers, the more compelling your messaging strategy will be. This can take some research in your industry and in your buyer's makeup to determine what sort of terminology they prefer, what tone of voice compels them to act, and what keywords they really respond to. Beyond that, focus on telling a good story. This makes your product memorable, and can also take a complex idea and turn it into a simple one. In our PawTastic Pup Treat example, we are aware that most consumers don't really want a scientific breakdown of everyone of our organic ingredients or the chemical breakdown of the dyes that can be so harmful in retail dog treats. What they do want is knowledge of the end result: What benefits the healthy treats give their dogs, and what sort of illnesses and diseases can be avoided by not consuming the treats that contain the extra chemicals and dyes. A simple animation or illustration can make this process a lot more relatable to the average person. Once you have this core story established that makes your brand memorable, create narratives that feed into it and customize your content so that your target audience is able to gain more and more knowledge on your story at different touch points along the process.

STEP FOUR: SOURCING AND MANAGING CONTENT

It does not take a rocket scientist to understand that the more valuable the content you produce the better it is for your brand. Content creation should not be a one-person job, it shouldn't even be a one-department job. Your content stream can come from both likely and unlikely stories including: your marketing and sales teams; any content writers you use regularly, whether they are full-time employees or freelance/ contractor types; other employees that might have a unique perspective on how your product comes to life; your customers; ad agencies; even crowdsourcing. Regardless of what source the content comes from, every piece of it should represent the best your brand has to offer. Once your audit is done and you've created a content schedule, the pressure can make it difficult not to rush creation for the sake of deadline, just like the desire to produce as much content as possible can see a glut of it form. Remember that more than anything else, quality is the most important characteristic your content must possess. Every piece should represent the best that your brand has to offer and deliver rich experiences to your customers that help move them across their journey towards a point where they want to acquire the value of your product.

STEP FIVE: START PUBLISHING

Finally! You might have wondered if this step would ever come, but now that it's here, you need to be prepared with the best tool at your disposal: the editorial calendar. Timing is a big deal here. You don't want to set such a frantic page that if your followers don't see something every 48 hours they jump ship, but you also don't want to have the same blog post sitting there for more than a week with nothing fresh in front of it. Pace yourself. Do some more research and see what are the best days of the week and times of day to publish content. Realize there are some universal truths that should be adhered to. Don't launch a new product on Monday morning at 9 a.m. on your website, because most of your followers will be at their jobs getting started on their work week or sifting through the 300 emails that came to their inbox over the weekend. Don't post a fantastic new video from how your product is made at 7 p.m. on Friday when most of your target audience is out enjoying their first dose of weekend entertainment.

Create your Content marketing Strategy:

CONTENT AUDIT	FOLLOW YOUR BVP	TARGET BUYER PERSONA	MANAGING CONTENT	PUBLISH

YOU CANNOT BUY ENGAGEMENT. YOU HAVE TO BUILD ENGAGEMENT.

Tara Nicholle Nelson

CHAPTER 6

DELIVERING YOUR MESSAGE

In the modern digital environment, flexibility is huge and knowing your audience is more important than ever. The Internet allows for far more cost-effective options than traditional marketing ever did. Those approaches simply cannot bring the same return on investment, nor the same quality of analytics that breaks down what's working and what's not. As more and more businesses successfully experiment with digital advertising, they're realizing that taking the broader multimedia branding route makes total sense in today's ultra-competitive marketing climate.

So what strategies should you employ? No new companies are alike, but there are plenty of tips and tricks that you can follow to make your campaigns a success.

The first of those is that you should not blow your budget on paid media. This is a blind man's strategy that no capable 21st century company should be handicapped by. Paying for ads and hoping for the best is antiquated. Data shows that customers are increasingly willing to pay a premium to avoid ads altogether - such as on streaming services like Netflix, paid cable networks, and music providers like Spotify. In July 2019, Netflix which has a flat-rate subscription but no commercials, announced that it had earned a 10% share of all screens in the US. If that does not smack of the end of traditional advertising as we once knew it, we don't know what does.

Instead of paid advertising, begin optimizing your own channels, ensuring that they are the ones that your target audience readily pays attention to and relies upon for decisions about what to spend money on. These can include blogs, websites, and social media to engage your audience. Add to that mix a good social sharing strategy as well as one for good content marketing. Your owned channels can generate far more attention and much better engagement than paid channels because your potential customers are already there looking for content relevant to their pain points and problems that need solutions.

We replace paid media with earned media as a way to really start cultivating a following and earning customers organically.

You can think of earned media as word of mouth on steroids. If the Internet has taught us one thing, it's that people trust peer recommendations such as shares, retweets, and user reviews far more than any other form of media.

Here are some key statistics concerning the rise of earned media and the decline of paid media:

38% of US adults have installed ad-blocking software on their computers, meaning paid Internet ads are being negated from even being seen by those consumers.

Only 47% of people trust the ads that appear alongside search engine results, while close to 92% trust online reviews.

81% of senior marketers believe earned media has more of a positive impact than paid media.

For some companies, paid media will always have its place. The Coca-Colas and Toyotas of the world use TV advertising to drive their overall branding and remind people of their significance. However, there is no doubt that a strategic focus on owned and earned media can inform, educate, and even entertain in ways that paid media simply can't.

For further analysis, we return to our example of PawTastic Pup Treats. Paid Internet ads might work on occasion for people searching for "organic dog treats", but there's no way we can outbid the likes of PetsMart and other big retailers except perhaps in very specific markets for the top spot. Advertising in print might work on a limited basis for any local pet-related magazines, but the radio and television are too general of populations to think even the slightest dent might appear.

That leaves digital media, and as we have discussed earlier in this chapter, social media and message boards are ideal homes for what we are trying to sell. Comparison videos of our treats against the generic equivalent can not only hit home with viewers but are easily shareable across social media and message boards, getting the word out to potential consumers like traditional media never could. Couple that with the ability to really connect with consumers via message boards, any number of which are driven by health-concerned pet owners looking to give their canines the best life possible. Starting conversations and topics there takes a certain skill to keep other participants to feel that you are there just to sell a product. You have to convey concern for their problems and present a solution in a very organic way. This is easier to do on social media, where most people are promoting something. Having a full range of business profiles for your product along Facebook, Twitter, Instagram, even 4Square if you have a brick-and-mortar location, can really augment those conversations and connections.

Remember that just because you have access to a lot of different options for media channels, does not mean you need to use them all. Your intended audience is going to have specific ways they like to be contacted. Just ask them if you want, they'll be more than happy to tell you all about it.

The automotive industry has seen this realized in force with the rise of YouTube's power as a sales comparison tool. Research showed that customers were spending less and less time at dealerships because it was far more convenient and easy to research cars online. Only about 5% of industry-related content online was coming from the actual dealerships, while YouTube was generating a larger and larger percentage. It's become such a trend that Tesla actually closed its dealerships so that customers can only order its cars online.

Once you select your channel remember to match your message to the media and focus on what makes your brand unique, and above all, be authentic. The problem is that every other good marketing department is trying to achieve the exact same thing that you are. And they are throwing everything they have into it just like you. The result is the average person getting exposed to hundreds of marketing messages every day. Our brains decide quickly whether to engage those messages or absolutely ignore them based on the content, voice, tone, etc. Your goal is to find the exact perfect touch to be engaging, but not intrusive.

Intrusion is one of the main problems with paid media. It is seen more as invasive instead of informative. Paid media ads are a tax that most consumers aren't interested in paying. They overstay their welcome, especially when they are bought in a format where they appear twice in close proximity to each other during a commercial break. At its best, paid media complements owned media. It should invite customers to learn more about owned media sources such as your website, YouTube channel, blogs and social media channels. What you're searching for in all this is the ability to balance your message across multiple channels in a way that allows you to stay ahead of the competition, use both qualitative and quantitative analysis to measure the effectiveness of your messaging, and also measure the media consumption habits of your audience members.

As essential and powerful all that Big Data can be, don't forget that the human connections remain the biggest part of your media plan. Forging meaningful connections allows you to keep building onto the initial relationships as well as building up your brand. Your audience will not only connect to that message, but pass it on in their social circles and professional networks, giving you the most valuable and least expensive forms of advertising you can find. Finding the connection, often through hitting on a particular emotional note and expanding it into a memorable story, is the real key to making this relationship work.

So you've integrated traditional media with your website, blogs, articles, and so on, now it's time to start thinking about social media and how to add it to the mix in a creative, intelligent way. One of the best parts about social media is that fresh minds are capable of using it in really unique ways. Celebrate those possibilities with your own brand, but when you need some surefire winners, here are a few things to consider:

Show what you stand for: If someone is following your brand on Twitter, Instagram, LinkedIn, or Facebook, you don't have to explain to them what you do. We're going to safely assume that if someone is following PawTastic Pup Treats on Twitter, they've already discerned that our company is selling dog treats. So instead of wasting precious time and attention, use these social networks to let viewers see what sort of things your company stands for. A great example comes from US-based Hershey's Chocolate. In 2015, it released a campaign focused on efforts to sustain the daily diets of more than 50,000 school-age children in Ghana. Obviously this was not a maneuver designed to sell more M&M's and Reese's Peanut Butter Cups, but to show that Hershey's is a company that thinks about more than simply lining its own pocketbook.

Focus on your content strategy: The brands with the best plans create the best content; it doesn't take a brain surgeon to put two and two together. Take a look at Intel. It is always improving its B2B content marketing game by ensuring that the content fits the platform. From there, they let the data do the talking, which typically drives B2B pieces. If an unpaid organic piece of content is doing great, then Intel pays to boost its reach, realizing that if the piece is something that a target audience wants to see, it's worth the funds to get it seen by as many people as possible.

Be respectful at all times: One of the toughest things to do when owning a business is treating everyone with respect, especially the people who are loudly criticizing or complaining about your business. If you lose your cool and lash out at a social media comment or a negative online, it will spread like wildfire across the Internet, even if you try to delete it 10 seconds later. This includes having a negative reaction to a bad review of your business. Think before you type anything, and if you think what you're saying might have the slightest bit of a negative connotation, take about 10 minutes before hitting "Post". Alternatively, have a team of gatekeepers in place to keep poorly-written or poorly-conceived social media messages or responses from representing you on the Internet. Social media should be used to share your experiences and authentic messages, along with conducting two-way exchanges between you and customers, potential customers, and potential partners. Be positive at all times on social media and never use it to cast negative emotions or feelings about anyone.

YOUR BRAND IS A STORY UNFOLDING ACROSS ALL CUSTOMER TOUCH POINTS.

Jonah Sachs

CHAPTER 7

CUSTOMER EXPERIENCE

If you're above a certain age, you've probably heard of the customer communication model known as AIDA. That's an acronym for Awareness, Interest, Desire, and Action. It came into existence in the early 20th century thanks to American sales pioneer E. St. Elmo Lewis. In its four-step process, AIDA showed consumers becoming aware of a product, usually through advertising; gaining interest by learning about brand benefits and how the brand fits with lifestyle; developing a favorable desire towards the brand, and ultimately forming an actionable purchase interest after shopping around or engaging in a trial, leading to a purchase. AIDA was the gold standard for a long time, but it's always been missing one thing: the customer experience.

That all changed when the McKinsey Model reared its head in the past decade, profiling the customer decision journey (abbreviated to CDJ). This is a mode that describes the process customers undergo before making any purchase decisions; it predicates there is no such thing as an impulse buy, the CDJ can be very quick or drawn out over time. Every purchase customers make is a decision journey, involving interactions with brands from the initial contact to the point of making a decision.

The McKinsey model, also known as the CDJ model, consists of four steps:

Consideration: Customers show interest in a number of brands, looking for the one that can fulfill their needs and solve their problems.

Active evaluation: Customers evaluate the brands they have shown interest in by accessing multiple databases of information. They reduce the number of brands in the running based on each ones pros and cons.

Buy: The customer purchases a brand based on their needs.

Post-purchase experience: The customer has used the product and can now gather experience on how well it functions. If they are fully satisfied, they may rate and recommend the product to others - this is the earned media we spoke about earlier. This type of word-of-mouth marketing forms the core of McKinsey's CDJ.

The CDJ works great with both B2B and B2C marketing. It's also proof positive that it takes more than just new tools and different engagement platforms to create a customer-centric brand; it takes a fundamental shift in mindset and strategy. At every step of the journey, the customer's experience matters more than anything else. But what does this look like and how does it work for your company?

The brand of the 21st century wants to appear as an ally to the consumer. This process starts by taking a human approach to both technology and business, with the goal of supporting the customer experience through their buying journey. Here are a few basic strategies to get your company into that role of advisor/confidante on the customer journey.

TAKE THE CUSTOMER JOURNEY

Want to design a seamless customer experience? Put yourself in their shoes and experience your brand as they do. You'll probably be surprised at what you learn. One of the toughest things for a company to do is see itself objectively, and this really holds water when it comes to the customer journey. Knowing the ends and outs of a business make it tough to really see it for what it is, but this is your chance to see through the eyes of your customers. We'll take it back to our experience with PawTastic Pup Treats. We pull ourselves out of the corporate mindset and into the realm of someone looking for a healthy, tasty, organic dog snack. We create a profile on a Southern California dog blog and message board and start surfing around various threads to see what they have to say about our own product. A few well-timed statements by our own employees get a healthy debate on what local companies are making the kind of snacks we're looking for. We don't want to self-promote too much or we'll look like plants, so we leave it to other users of the forum to spread the word about where to find us on the Internet or social media. Unfortunately, that plan goes awry when another user mistakenly links our name to a website for a company called PupTastic Dog Treats located in Australia. Now while a few endeavoring users might go to the wrong site, realize the mistake, and Google their way to us, the majority will see it's the wrong site and jump off to some other destination. Just like that, our customer journey has gone astray, and we have to reconsider how to get users where we want them to go by being a bit more vociferous about where we're located. So let's say we fix that glitch and send them to our website. They get a good look around the place, notice some of our videos and infographics, and move to the blog page. But we're so focused on social media that we haven't updated our blog in three months. Since we're a fairly new business, the customer could rightly assume we've gone out of business or we're not really that sincere about helping the customer, since this channel is out of date. Mistake #2! We update the blog page and give the customer the right to share our info easily. That turns them onto our social media accounts where they can really engage with us and see how active we are in the local community. At last, they are getting the full extent of the customer journey.

SIMPLIFY

For a long time, consumer electronics came with increasingly complicated user interfaces. That didn't make much sense to anyone. With the rise of smartphones and tablets, however, users can do just about anything with the tap of a button or the swipe of a finger. The lesson here is that sometimes sophistication isn't about adding more; but rather about minimizing things to highlight your core value. Too complicated? Our dog treat example comes to the rescue once more. The core value there is that our dog treats are tasty, safe, and healthy for your dog. The process we use to manufacture them is fairly complex, because it involves circumventing commonly used ingredients like moisture, artificial colors, and preservatives. Unless you were majoring in nutrition, the odds that you could understand, much less be interested in reading all about that process, are very little. But the step-by-step manufacturing process is not a core value for us; providing your pet with healthy, delicious snacks is. All the rest of that process exists, but it can be sheared down to get to the really important parts of the process. We might have all the digital technology in the world to dazzle a user during their journey, but the plain simple truth is all we want them to see.

ALWAYS BE INNOVATING

Never rest on your laurels, no matter how successful your customer journey experience is. Keep collaborating and experimenting to push the product forward towards the next big thing. History is full of examples of companies that thought they had captured lightning in a bottle, only to realize it was short-lived. Make sure you have a well-versed technical person on staff to keep you abreast of what's next and now in the IT world. Imagine being the company that realized belatedly that everyone else had developed an app for their brand before you did. Or that other companies were putting smart sensors in their stores to see exactly what objects customers are touching and talking about. It can be difficult to lock in on the future when the present is where you're making your connections, customers, and revenue. But it's absolutely essential to stay ahead of the competition. Better to fail early on the next best thing then hear about it three months after everyone else has converted.

Optimizing your brand experience is a constant thing. A big reminder is that in this digital environment we're all living in, the best ideas don't necessarily come from the creatives in marketing and sales. Almost every employee who works in the online environment has had previous experience doing something creative, and it's surprising how many times someone else has the idea that sends you veering in an unexpected but quite pleasant direction. No matter if your staff is made up of five people or 500, a great idea is to have a once-a-month or once-a-quarter brainstorming/crowdsourcing/hack-a-thon type event. At these, you can allow employees to cast aside their regular roles and responsibilities in favor of doing some old-fashioned, sleeves-rolled-up idea generation. Employees are often a lot more than their current roles in your company, and this is not only a great way to see what they've got in mind, but a good trial run for promoting them to a different position at some point. Companies like Facebook and Google are famous for this kind of event, and usually attach monetary or status awards to them as well.

Remember that not every idea pans out, but keep testing on the ones that hold some interest or some value. And don't forget to get input from your customers; some of the best ideas in business history have come from users who cared so passionately around a brand that they were able to craft the perfect system to help it advance. Check your ego at the door and get to work on finding the best ideas, regardless of the source.

At the end of the day, the best brands work to guide the journey through helpful content, thoughtful product design and support, and superior customer service. If you're just getting started on a new customer journey, here's a few tips that will keep customers coming back for more.

PUT YOUR CORE STORY EVERYWHERE

You crafted this core story for a reason - to define your business, your brand, who you are and what your product is. Don't shy away from it now! You might be a little tired of hearing the details of your brand-defining story, but that's because you work there. Most consumers are getting just snippets of it and are nowhere near committing it to memory. But that core story is your biggest selling point, so the more you can distribute it, the better. Think about the kind of automobile you drive. At the time you bought it, you probably knew a lot more about its brand than you do right now. You had watched lots of videos about it, read consumer reports, went on the brand's website a dozen times to compare options, took a test drive with a salesman, and read the brochure 30 times that tells you all about its quality engineering and impressive testing. That core story is designed to turn you into a paying customer. A few years later, only have a general recollection of those core values despite spending upwards of $30,000 on your vehicle. Keep pushing your core values through as many forms of media as your target audience allows for.

PROVIDE YOUR CUSTOMERS A PAINLESS JOURNEY

Have you ever taken a business trip only to find that your smooth path to the airport is stuffed with traffic and almost you missed the flight? It happens to all of us, but we can do our very best to avoid customers have that same problem. Streamline the personal journey to avoid things like broken links, slow-loading pages, or anything that is not responsive. You are the architect of this marketing plan, and the directions you point your users are entirely up to you. It's not just about the technical side of things, either. Ensure that the waypoints along the customer journey are easy to navigate and follow. It is worth noting here that the modern customer journey rarely travels in a state line. That means there are more ways to attract a new client than before, most of them will be a mix-and-match system designed by the clients themselves. That's why you can never scrimp when it comes to your content. The message should be just as vibrant on your website landing page as it is in 140 characters or less on Twitter.

ENFORCE THE EMOTIONAL CONNECTION

Whether you're aiming for nostalgia, happiness, problem-solving, organizational, or any other sort of opinion about your product or service, establishing it in the customer's mind and holding it there is job one, whether you're a B2B or B2C business. Sharing your brand's story is a great way to start connecting on a human level. Celebrate communities of shared interests and prove that customer satisfaction matters more than your bottom line.

In the end, your focus must be on helping your customers. Whether you build private jets or sell packs of gum, you have to show them how your brand can supplement their efforts to achieve what they need. Very rare is the product where customers can simply look at a picture and know that's the one for them. That means you'll have to create great content to push your brand to the head of the pack. And it doesn't stop with the things you write and share before the sale. Helping customers get the most out of their experience with your brand also means helping them make a first-time purchase, troubleshooting issues after the fact, and giving them a platform to provide feedback not only to you, but also for other customers that come after them. There's so much more to selling a product or service than what it does. You have to make the customer aware of the elements that set your product apart from the competition, connect them to the emotions of the story that drive your product, sell them on your own story, and get them to relate to the vision that you have for your company.

Doing so, and really mastering what the MBS strategy is all about, is reaching that right person with the right message at the right buying time in the right environment. As we've seen in these first seven chapters, that involves a dazzling array of choices and considerations, not only in building our product's value, but also in determining what path the customer journey will follow, what channels we will engage customers on, and what core messages we seek to convey each time they reach a touchpoint in the customer journey process.

It might seem like a long haul and a tricky, winding path, but it's also one fraught with opportunities that the small-to-medium size companies did not have in generations past. More than anything, the new look of the customer journey, with the ability for spreading information via earned and organic media, levels the playing field between the great and small companies of the world like little else before it has. This is the start of the era of business in which your brand is defined by those who experience it. The best experiences don't happen by accident, but through a process called Alignment, which we will explore later in this book. This is where you align your business goals with customer needs and behaviors in order to get in sync and experience a synergy that puts ourselves and our customers on the same wavelength. As we will see going forward, doing this allows us to improve their experience in a way that improves our own. Happier customers equals more opportunities for company growth, more revenue streams, and the ability to expand on that solid base in a number of different directions, pushing forward toward your vision of the future.

SECTION TWO: SALES

BECOME THE PERSON WHO WOULD ATTRACT THE RESULTS YOU SEEK.

Jim Cathcart

CHAPTER 8

THE POWER OF SOFT SELL SKILLS

It's time to elevate your sales game.

Let me tell you the story of Wilson and Peter. Two salespeople who are both successful in very different ways.

Wilson's success can be measured in numbers. It's all right there in front of you. When he sees new customers coming his way, he puts on his best smile, extends his best foot forward and gives them the best pitch they've heard all day. He's friendly and knowledgeable and quick with a joke and a knowing grin, but in his head he's also running the numbers: How much longer to close this sale? How many more can he squeeze in before lunch? How many more does he need to hit his monthly quota? How many more to buy that beach house he's got his eye on?

The bosses love Wilson and the bosses' bosses really love him because they're all about the numbers themselves. Every unit they sell is another dollar in the bank. The customer? He might remember Wilson two years later, but again he might not. Wilson has a lot of great qualities in a salesman that his superiors admire, but customers are looking for more than a quick pitch and a firm handshake these days.

Sales success has grown beyond hard sale skills. Product knowledge is incredibly essential these days. You've got to know your stuff backwards, forwards, and sideways, and know your competitors' stuff just as well. The Internet has given everyone access to an amazing amount of information on just about every product and service in the world. Plenty of customers come into a meeting with a salesperson having done an extensive amount of research, which leads them to a lot of deep questions, not just the standard: What size does it come in or what colors are available? It's OK to look up details now and again as a salesman, but knowing your products is a huge sign of strength when dealing face-to-face with customers.

But all of that is more on the technical side. What you really need to succeed in today's business world are soft sales skills, which are hard-to-define relational skills that give you the last true competitive edge in sales in the modern atmosphere.

You can sort of define soft sale skills as interpersonal relationship skills, although a salesman like Wilson has plenty of those as well. Soft sales skills experts could be prepared to a counselor or a psychologist - they know how to read the people they are dealing with, understand what their pain points are, show empathy in what is holding that person back from making a purchase, and guide them through the customer experience to the point of making a purchase they feel great about. If that sounds a lot like the online customer experience we talked about earlier in this book, you're on the right track. Now that we've talked a little about soft sales skills, let's meet our second successful salesman, Peter.

A few years back, after much hemming and hawing, I knew it was time for me to finally get a new car. I love holding onto my cars as long as I can because I want to get my money's worth on the payment process. Whether your car loan is 36 months, 48 months, or 60 months, there's no better feeling than getting to the end of it and using that monthly fixed rate to pay down other accounts or buy more of the things you really want.

Anyway, my car had hit 150,000 Km and was starting to get worn down so I made the decision to invest in a new vehicle. I made plans to sacrifice an otherwise relaxing Saturday to hit the streets. I went to several different dealers, saw a lot of different cars, talked to a bunch of sales people, and read a lot of reviews on my phone, but at the end of the day I just could not take the next step and make a final decision. I was frustrated, and I have no doubt the sales staff I spoke to was just as frustrated with me.

A few days later I was heading home from the office and saw another car dealership just ahead. It was one I had not been to before, so I decided to give it a try and see if I was any closer to making a choice. I was hoping that 48 hours of downtime since my all-day ordeal would have calmed my nerves and given me a chance to recover and regain my perspective on the process and the end result.

That's when I met Peter. That was the sales guy who walked over and casually introduced himself as I was gazing at a floor model vehicle. Right away, I could tell there was something different about him compared to the hustle-and-bustle salesmen I had largely dealt with on the previous Saturday. For starters, he seemed to be able to sense my concern about the investment I was going to be putting into the car. That by itself was a huge sign that I was dealing with someone who was viewing me as an actual person, not a number. A "close-the-deal" type of salesman won't worry much about you and where your money comes from, they just assume you have enough to pay or you wouldn't have walked through the door in the first place, right?

If Peter was feeling that way, he definitely had me fooled. Instead of trying to upsell me on options and extras, he took a considerable amount of time to figure out what I needed in a car, why I needed it, and what my biggest concerns regarding the purchase were. He didn't go with the round-hole, square-peg approach and try to cram all my wants into a car that was on the lot. No, he took down my information and told me he had some work to do. And work he did! In fact it was a full five days until he contacted me to tell me he had found the car that I really wanted that matched my needs and nailed my price. He didn't sell me a car. He solved my pain points and made it personal.

The next time someone asked me if I had any recommendations on an honest car salesman, I gave Peter's name without a moment's hesitation. And the time after that, and the time after that. When the automated feature called on the phone asking for a review of Peter's performance, I took the time and gave one of the most glowing testimonials you can imagine. And the next time I needed a new car, he was the first person I contacted. I've bought several vehicles over the last decade or so, and he's gotten the commission on every one of them.

Wilson is a great salesman. Peter is what we call an amazing salesman because he overdelivers. He not only is a master of technical sales skills, like finding the best interest rates and the best terms for my car loan, but he's a master of soft-selling skills. At no point during the process did I feel like Peter was pressuring me to make a decision. What he did was work step by step to get me from feeling uncomfortable about purchasing a car that didn't fit my budget nor my needs to finding that car and creating that solution based on his conversations with me, which were real, organic, and created the base of a real relationship between us that has now lasted for years.

His needs as a salesman - closing deals and making money for his company- became secondary to the needs of the customer. In the short term, spending five days to convert one customer would seem like lunacy to some salespeople. But to Peter, who cares about each customer and realizes the value of an incredible customer who becomes not only a repeat customer but also a source of referrals, it's well worth the investment of time.

Hard Skills + Soft Skills = Success

We've talked about hard-sell skills, technical skills, and soft-sell skills. Those are all broad-based terms when it comes to being a salesman, and pose an important question: What skills does the modern sales professional really need?

The modern economy, the evolving customer, and the overwhelming shift in technology have all changed the game in the world of selling. The era of cold calling, door-to-door salesmen, and simply expecting the customer to conform to what you're selling are gone. In these times of consumer fickleness, extreme marketplace shifts, and hyper-competition, how do you quantify the full range of sales skills that you need to succeed?

As we've seen above in my experience with Peter and buying a car, there are two broad skills that the modern salesperson must embody: A marketing component which allows the salesperson to drive (no pun intended) the customer through their purchase journey and a sales component which accountable for closing the sale. There can be quite a delicate balance between the two. The salesman can be exceptionally friendly with the customer and form an amazing relationship, but his first loyalty lies with his company. Moreover, he must realize that the hard sell skills he likely learned in sales training are now just one-half of what his job entails.

When we're talking hard skills, we're referring to things like CRM software management, goal-setting, product knowledge, and the industry-specific skills that set you apart from the rest of the business environment, whether you're selling cars, jet engines, organic dog treats, or flagpoles. This book does not focus on hard skills. Sales systems, lead quality, the art of negotiation, and like skills are not set in stone, but they are much more objective than soft skills.

Soft skills include relationship-building, those qualities and tactics that not only encourage your prospects to be interested in you, but to like you, trust you, and ultimately value your opinion and insight as you lead them on the customer journey. For some people, soft skills come as naturally as riding a bicycle does. For others, the hard skills are the ones that seem effortless. Rare is the salesman who can do both without first putting in some real elbow grease to hone his performance. But that's what you'll have to do to really rise above the rest of the thick competition. Not only do you have to have both exceptional hard and soft selling skills, but you need to integrate them flawlessly and know when it's time to use which one.

MAKE A CUSTOMER,
NOT A SALE.

Katherine Barchetti

CHAPTER 9

TOP FIVE SOFT SKILLS FOR TODAY'S SALES PROFESSIONAL

Are there only five soft skills you need to learn? Of course not, but these five will serve as a great foundation on which to build your sales persona, depending on who your audience is, where you are located geographically, and what industry you are selling in.

Here are our Big Five:

EMPATHY

This is where the test of if you are genuine or not will really come to light. It centers on how well you not only listen, but also understand the challenges your customers are facing.

This isn't patting them on the shoulder and telling them everything will be OK - that's sympathy, and not what most clients want. It's not a look you want to affect either, being sympathetic to a customer's needs can make you look like you're talking down to them. You want to present yourself as on the same level as the customer, not a superior being granting them a favor. Can you see the sales experience from the customer's point of view? And can you continue to adapt to that point of view as you move from customer to customer? Let's think back to my one-of-a-kind auto salesman Peter. When he met me, he was able to use his soft selling skills to see that my biggest pain point was the investment I was making and whether or not the return on it in terms of the things I wanted and expected from a car would be worth that investment. He did not criticize or mock me for pinching my pennies, he was able to get into the mindset that value was the problem I needed solving and make it a problem that he understood and could solve.

The next day, Peter might have encountered a customer who wanted a car that would reflect his perceived social/ professional status as an trend-setter and an industry leader. The average salesperson would have tried to get this customer into a luxury automobile or a flashy sports car, but Peter is the kind of salesman who really listens to what the customer is saying. For a customer like this, the price is not nearly as important as it was for me. This customer wants something unique in his car; something that will make others stop and stare at the vehicle and want to see who the man or woman is who gets out when the door opens. To make that happen, Peter would do his research and educate himself on special features and options that could give the customer a one-of-a-kind or exclusive vehicle that either no one or almost no one else on the road had. Maybe the manufacturer put out a special touring model or a racing model that is available in limited numbers. Perhaps there are certain rare colors of the car available only in small quantities. Maybe there is a features package that turns the car into the equivalent of a mobile entertainment center with WiFi, DVD players, the best stereo on the market, etc. Empathy is the ability to not just make that connection with a few customers, but with every customer, to the point where every new connection is both a challenge and an opportunity.

CONNECTION

Being able to make a connection to your customers or potential customers is perhaps the hardest of the soft sells skills to learn if aren't naturally blessed with it. It's the intangible measurement that cannot be faked or forced, and if you try, you run the risk of really alienating your customer and turning them off from you as a source of knowledge or trust. How do you form a connection? You find a commonality between you and the customer and make it into a touchstone that you return to at key points during the customer's journey. A key thing to remember that many "by the numbers" sales professional struggle to grasp is that the connection does not have to have a single thing to do with the item or service you're trying to sell. In fact you might go entire days talking to the customer and never even mention the item or service by name! The connection can be literally anything, from attending the same high school to liking the same baseball team to being the mother of twins. Forming a connection over the product or service in question is also quite possible, but that usually comes farther along the line of the customer experience. For now, we're looking for something besides what you're trying to sell them to be the foundation of your relationship.

As mentioned in the lead, forging connections is very tough because doing it disingenuously can be worse than not doing it at all. If a client walks into a meeting wearing the colors of a popular football squad, don't immediately proclaim yourself their biggest fan if you're not. Ask leading questions that will let the customers talk about themselves, and as they talk, look for commonalities between your life and interests and theirs. It could be that they're the oldest of several children, or the youngest. Perhaps they or their parents have a military background. Start at the surface and dig down a bit deeper as the opportunity presents itself. And beyond that, strive to be more well-rounded so that you know enough about a lot of subjects to talk about them intelligently if they come up.

Also remember that having a connection does not mean you have to milk it to death. If you both have a certain favorite restaurant in the area, don't bring it up each and every time you talk to them. Pushing the issue over and over will make the wrong impression on your clients, making them feel you're using something they like as a leverage point to get your business. And remember, the connection does not have to be something you both like. Customers are not all going to be happy, go-lucky individuals. Some will come in stressed from work, from a bad relationship, from economics struggles at home or at the office, etc. Connections come from a wide range of emotional responses. When you're listening and engaging your customers, you are much more likely to hear those connections form.

LISTENING

For some salespeople, the idea of listening instead of talking is about as logical as staring straight into the sun: How can they possibly get their point across and deliver their winning pitch if their mouths are closed? This sort of soft skill defies a lot of old-school tactics about commanding the conversation, directing the flow of it, and so on, but it's one the most definitive of soft skills when it comes to adapting to what the modern customer looks like and wants. Let's face it: The average customer isn't simply wandering into your location or visiting your website with no idea what they want. As we've mentioned earlier, they'll have done some research on your industry and the specific product or service they're interested in and have some pointed questions that they want answered by you, the industry professional. That initial minute of conversation is a great look into their mindset because they're going to be laying a lot of what they are looking for out there, if you simply close your mouth and listen. And there's definitely more to it than just the words they say, but how they say them, what their posture is like, what sort of body language they use, and more. Some customers aren't ready to give you all their details, they want to see what kind of deal and how much information they can pilfer from you first before explaining the whole story.

When you're listening to a customer, you're seeking out several points of data including:

Why do they want to make a purchase?

What is their time frame for making a purchase?

What is their price point for the purchase?

What obstacles are keeping them from making the purchase?

What information are they seeking to complete their knowledge of the product/service?

Most of that information a customer will readily tell you. Some of it, like the price point, they might hold in reserve until near the end of the customer journey, as they fear it might price them out of what they want to purchase. Don't push too hard on that point, let the customer take the lead as they detail the things that are most important to them. Never talk over the customer - not only is it rude, but it can make you miss vital details they are trying to pass on to you. Of course, the situation can also go the other way with a client that has no idea what they want or what is limiting them from making a purchase. In these cases, your job is to find those answers and listening is perhaps more important than ever, as their responses to your queries will form the framework of your relationship and how you can best satisfy their wants/needs.

COMMUNICATION

Listening leads to communication. Give and take. Question and answer. It is a balance and an artform that combines your ability to hear the customer's questions and concerns and respond to them appropriately to move them forward organically on their customer journey. This is the soft sales skill that a lot of salespeople fumble. They try to funnel all of their responses through the filter of getting the customer to buy a product as quickly as possible to close the sale and move on to the next lead. As mentioned previously, people are much more perceptive than they are often given credit for by veteran sales staff. When a customer engages you in conversation about a purchase, there's nothing more important to them in that moment than getting the information necessary to help them make a decision. If you are conveying the attitude or body language that you want to get the sale done as quickly as possible so you can get to the next one, back to the break room, or out to lunch, the sale will be gone before it even begins. You might have a standard sales pitch or two that works for a majority of your customers, but the individual communication should be the real inspiration for customizing those messages to the person in front of you at the time. Use what they say to create a story that sells the product they need. While a lot of customers can be grouped into the larger population of people who want a great product for a great price, there are infinite subsets within and beyond that group that your soft sell skills must account for in order to please the person right in front of you and turn them into a long-time, repeat customer who is more than willing to organically pass on and promote your skills as a salesman.

RELATIONSHIP BUILDING

This is a long-term goal and not something you can rush. Most times it has nothing to do with an actual sale, it's reaching out to let them know you're invested in their satisfaction with their purchase and on standby if they ever need anything else. You also need to practice this with the members of the team to let them know you care about them and their success all the time, not just when it suits your needs to close a deal. Consider it much like you would making a new friend. If you ride the elliptical bike at work next to another person and end up talking sports with them for an hour, you'll probably look forward to doing something similar with them the next time you are both there, or you might even grab coffee or lunch after the workout. But you're not going to introduce them to your whole family and extend an invitation to come over for Christmas lunch after one workout. Customer relationships are the same way. You start with one interaction and build on it from there. You get to know them as more than just a customer, and let them know you as more than just a salesman, whatever that looks like - common interests, talking about your families, etc. The more familiar you get, the more the customer will view you as something beyond a salesman and more of a familiar face they can rely on when they need something. When they begin to refer to you by your first name instead of by the company you work for, that's when you know you're doing things right. Over time, you can cultivate a relationship built on trust and the ability to provide them solutions to their problems. This is the same message for your team members, since success today is much more of a team effort. The more you invest in others, the more they will invest in you.

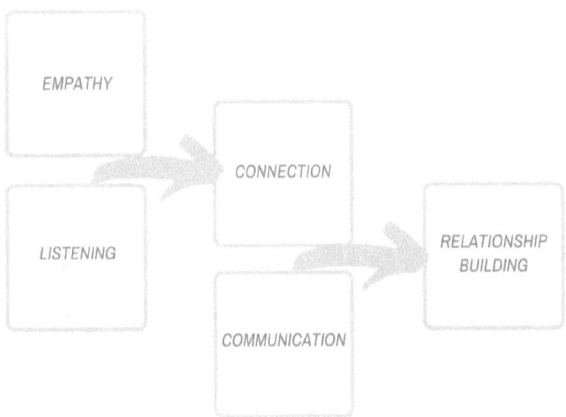

WHEN REPS TAKE THE ROLE OF A CURIOUS STUDENT RATHER THAN AN INFORMED EXPERT, BUYERS ARE MUCH MORE INCLINED TO ENGAGE.

Jeff Hoffman

CHAPTER 10

EMPATHY AND CONNECTION GET RESULTS

Showing empathy and making connections might not jibe with the way you've always handled your sales. If you prefer hard numbers to words in a book, consider this.

According to a study by Development Economics, sales professionals who excel at the soft skills found they outperform their competitors by more than 30%, and outperform them in areas such as close ratio, size of sales, and customer retention. Thirty percent! That means if you're doing $5,000 in sales per week, the soft-skills guru is making $6,500 in the same week. Extrapolate that out a bit and it means they're outperforming you by $6,000 per month, $18,000 per quarter, and $72,000 per year. Got your attention, yet?

In today's marketplace, soft skills allow us to attract new customers, deepen and expand existing relationships (both customers and coworkers), and advancing our own careers. Believing otherwise is a dangerous proposition, especially when dealing with customers. Consider that with almost no exceptions, a customer can go online and buy just about any product they want to without having to engage a salesman at all. That goes for everything from a shirt to a couch to a car. Scary, right?

And while there are customers who make a majority of their purchases online, very few of them are 100% comfortable with doing so. When they are buying something big, important, or unfamiliar, most would much rather deal with an actual person than a website or a chatbot.

But it's not just any type of salesperson they want to engage with, it's the kind who makes them feel comfortable, who doesn't insult their intelligence, who takes everything they're saying very seriously, and who is committed to giving them the best possible fit based on dialogue.

To prove this point, think of the last sales rep who really got on your nerves. It might have been a customer service rep that kept asking you personal questions when all you really wanted was to see if a wooden table came in a different color or a saleswoman who kept trying to upsell you when you'd already made your budget clear. These people can be so irritating, and often so unaware of it, that you just want to walk away from the sale.

In a sales experience, it's the little things that make the biggest difference, and done properly, those little things are driven and controlled by a salesperson's soft skills. My opinion is, and has been for years, that soft skills are the only competitive advantage we have left. With rare exception, no matter how unique, spectacular, or amazing your product or service might be, your customer just thinks of it as a commodity, something they can purchase anywhere, anytime, and from anyone else just as easily as from you. That means that unless you can quantify yourself as valuable, you are disposable to the customer's mindset. That means that it's ultimately not what you sell but how you sell it that's going to make the biggest difference. Your skills are the path that people take to get to know you, like you, and trust you. Ultimately, your customers are buying you, not the product.

Let's take a look at an example that can really clarify the difference between a salesperson and a soft-skills salesperson.

I was contacted by a gentleman named Nick who was in the market for some new equipment. We hammered everything out on the phone over the course of a few days and he scheduled an appointment to come to my office to sign the papers and finalize the deal. When he came in, we exchanged pleasantries, I got him some coffee, and we headed for my office to go over the paperwork.

I could tell from his body language and facial expression that something was amiss, and he told me, "Actually, I was talking to my team and we're having some second thoughts. We feel if we tighten our schedule a bit and optimise the outsourcing of extra costs for the next year or so, we can probably do without this equipment right now."

In that moment, the decision becomes mine on how to pursue the manner. I know that he and his company's minds clearly aren't all the way made up about not buying the equipment, or he wouldn't have come all the way to my office for the meeting, he could have simply told me over the phone or via email. That means that the sale is not gone, but it's no longer a sure thing either. It's in limbo, but with the customer right in front of me, the sale is no longer the most important thing: a happy, satisfied, customer is.

If my only goal at this point was to close the deal, I could have responded by saying, "OK, Nick, I understand, but I have the paperwork ready, and you did say you were coming in to sign it. It's normal to get cold feet before a bi decision, but remember the reasons you made the decision in the first place. It was the right one then and it's the right one now. I think we should move ahead."

I could have even embellished that opinion by handing him my fancy fountain pen and turning the contract to the page where I had pre-marked the line I needed him to sign on. And to be honest? There's a pretty good chance it would have worked, and he would have signed it. He was clearly in a mindstate where he wanted me to help him make the right decision. If I had pushed him towards signing, it's likely he would have given in.

But that would fly in the face of everything I believe in and everything I've been teaching in this book and elsewhere. What would be the impact if I replied to Nick that way without any empathy at all? From the customer's perspective, it would seem like I was just pushing to close the deal. Imagine how that would make him feel, especially if we had been previously cultivating a customer-client relationship. Everything I would have previously said about taking care of the customer would have seemed phony. Even if he did sign the papers that day, the likelihood of him ever calling me for another deal would have been slim to none.

But, of course, that's not the reply I used. Instead I slid the stack of papers back to the corner of my desk and turned my full attention to Nick and the statement he had just made. Instead, I said: "Okay Nick, that's interesting. Tell me more. In fact, walk me through exactly how that would work. I'll play Devil's advocate so we can be sure you're making the right decision."

So he laid out the company's ideas and concerns. We went through pros and cons together of several different situations and what that would look like with or without the equipment. By the end of our talk, we had a mutual understanding on the real challenges this company was facing. I told him to think it over, talk to his coworkers, and call me with any questions. I didn't say a word about the pre-existing contract or tell him to call me when he was ready to buy. I left it completely open-ended with my only request is that he takes his time and reach out for questions.

The day after that he called me, came in, and signed the contract. That's the beauty of empathy. Rather than pushing for the close, I backed up tried to understand where he was coming from and made him feel like his opinion and himself were important, understood, and valued.

Hearing a client reconsider at the last minute can often lead to internal freakouts by salespeople who are so focused on the bottom line and fearful of losing a sale. But that's the paradigm shift that really sets soft sales skills apart: Making the customer more comfortable and in a more positive state of mind are more likely to close the deal rather than just selling them from a script and getting to the finish line as quickly as possible.

YOU CAN'T PROPOSE A MUTUALLY BENEFICIAL BUSINESS RELATIONSHIP IF YOU CAN'T UNDERSTAND THEIR BUSINESS.

Craig Rosenberg

CHAPTER 11

CONNECTION AND LISTENING GET RESULTS

When it comes to sales training, it's a lot easier both to teach and to learn how to make a great sales presentation or how to use a certain kind of customer relationship management (CRM) system to track and record your calls than it is to pick up the nuances of soft skills. That's one of the reasons they often get overlooked; sales managers just assume they are part of some intrinsic skill set that every salesman possesses. Soft sales skills are not black and white and not nearly as straightforward to teach or to learn. It's true that some sales professionals are more naturally inclined to use and succeed with soft skills, but that does not mean others should not make the same attempt. No matter your natural levels of talent, soft skills can be learned. From there, you'll be in a constant state of cultivating them: practicing whenever you can, seeing what works and what doesn't, and turning weaknesses into strengths.

But where to start? Know the skills first from our list of five above and break them down based on how well they apply to your sales role. This will help you focus on the most effective skills first. If they happen to be the ones you have a natural affinity for, you can start trying them out with customers and others to see how well they fit into your sales experience.

And like for the marketing it is necessary to understand the why first, why it matters, why it's important, and why and how it will impact the outcome of your sale. It's not enough to know what the skills are, you need to know why they are important to your particular salesmanship.

The most effective way to learn soft skills is to engage in role play activities. Setting up scenarios gives you the opportunity to put your soft skills into action in an environment where you can really develop them without fear of failure. Use coworkers, friends, and family members to help you, but you can't just dive right in. Both for the roleplay environment and for your actual sales, you'll need a framework, which means an organization of your critical thinking and problem-solving skills. The framework will be the way you access the tools you need for each customer you have. Not all sales are the same, and need different approaches to be done right. Some are simple and straightforward; others are complex like a jigsaw puzzle with a ton of missing pieces. You have to develop the skills to understand how to solve each one. You can have all the product knowledge in the world, but if you cannot add value or personalize the experience for the customer, your chances of success drop.

Every customer in every industry in the world has a different story, a different set of problems that need solving, and a different set of solutions that will satisfy them and make them happy. Even if one customer's story sounds very similar to another who you dealt with recently, you need to explore every angle and hang on every word to give them the best analysis to tailor a unique solution.

Here's a step-by-step process to follow that can serve as a great baseline guide as you start incorporating all this into your sales process.

We are in the interrogative/investigative phase. We need to ask questions to find out why the customer needs our service or product, but more importantly what is driving them to pursue a resolution. Getting something new is on their minds; we don't have to push any further at this point. This is all about listening. Listening gives us the opportunity to analyze what was actually said rather than going to the next section of our script, which usually veers the conversation off in a different direction that has nothing to do with the conversation.

Next comes the clarification. You take what the customer has told you and tell it back to them as you understand it. This has two results. One, it confirms that you heard what the customer said, and two, it lets them know you were listening. Clarification and understanding are enormous techniques for trust building.

Third, the salesman creates and explains alternatives. This creates the power of choice for the customer, which is a very important mental process. Ever been to a store and been told by a clerk that "This is the only thing we have?" Unless you're desperately in need of whatever the object is, this is usually a signal to find a better store with more selection (and a friendlier staff). It also gives the customer the feeling of ownership of the sale. By providing multiple options or more than one solution, you're giving them the freedom to explore, ask more questions, and take their time. If you can't think of another solution off the top of your head, tell the customer you would like to consult with your team about it. Make sure you give the customer a set date and time that works for them for your next meeting in order to keep the momentum going and keep them progressing on the customer journey. And don't just use your "consult with the team" as an excuse, really tap their minds and see what they can come up with given the parameters you've laid out for them based on what your customer said. The best idea does not have to come from your mind for it to work for the customer. The sales process is so much more than taking orders and signing paperwork. Use empathy and really put yourself into your customer's situation, then use your own knowledge of your product/service to deduce where the two intersect and how to make that work for the customer.

Here's a quick example to show you how this works for a salesman and a store. Several months ago, my family decided to put in one of those video-camera doorbell systems so that when the doorbell rings or someone approaches your front door, you get a chime on your phone. You can access the camera and see who is there, and even talk to them through a built-in microphone/speaker. When dealing with solicitors, it is a great way to let them know you are not interested. If someone is walking around looking for houses to rob, it's a great way to let them know that not only are you home, but you are watching them.

The system is fairly simple to install, covering up your own existing doorbell, but it needs a few hand tools, including a power drill, to do so. I'm not the handiest guy in the world, but I endeavored to do it myself and headed for the local chain hardware store to buy a drill. I didn't know what I was looking for, how big it should be, what the best brand, or anything else like that. My only goal was to find a salesman who could identify the size of drill bit that came with the hardware for the doorbell system and see what the least-expensive drill was that could get the job done.

That was my entire presentation to the sales staff member who came over to help me. He identified the size of drill bit and started looking through the adjacent power drills when a thought occurred to him and he turned back to me.

"How often do you use a drill?" he asked. I told him this would be the second time ever and the first time was more than 10 years ago. "You're not installing anything else? You're not doing any Do it Yourself stuff?" I said that I was not.

He took my answers, analyzed them, and told me that it would be a waste of my money to buy a brand-new drill, and that his store could lend me one for around $35 for 4-6 hours. All I would have to do was pay a deposit and return the drill in the same condition I got it within that time frame. He walked me over to the tool rental department, explained my situation to his coworker and told me to have a good day.

And not only did I get the right drill, but since it was for rent and not for sale, the rental representative was able to show me how to sit the drill bits in the drill and show me how the basic controls worked before sending me on my way. Let's backtrack to the salesman for a minute. I gave him the knowledge that I did not know the first thing about drills. He could have easily recommended any from the smallest to the biggest, told me it was the essential solution, and pocketed a nice commission. But instead he looked at me and my specific needs: a drill to do a one-time job. From that, he created the alternative solution. Instead of spending $100 for a drill that would sit on a shelf after today, I could spend $35, learn how to use it in-store, and get my installation done and never worry about the drill again. It was the perfect custom solution just for me and it worked like a charm. My trust level for the store and its brand skyrocketed because they found the perfect solution for me inside my knowledge base and price range.

SALES IS NOT ABOUT SELLING ANYMORE, BUT ABOUT BUILDING TRUST AND EDUCATING.

Siva Devaki

CHAPTER 12

COMMUNICATION AND RELATIONSHIP BUILDING

Having a customer who won't talk to you is almost as bad as being the doctor of a patient who cannot speak. If they can't tell you what is wrong, how can you make it right? You can be the slickest salesman in your department, know the product guide front and back, have the perfect closing speech, the whole nine yards, but if you cannot use the soft skills: get clients to open up, share information, relate to them to see what's causing the problem, discuss their fears, and get ahold of their biggest challenges, then you will never be able to sell to them in the way that you want to. It is a simple 21st century fact: the stronger your communication skills, the easier and more effective your sales process will be from end to end. You have to know your communication style and be able to adapt it to the communication style of your customer. No distractions! No smartphone out to check your 6 million personal messages flooding in every 20 seconds. Fully engaged must be your mindset and the look of you when you are engaged with a customer. Nobody else is more important than the person you are in front of or on the phone with. If you think you can balance them with another customer, remember, you are not a professional juggler. All you're going to do is drop everything and make a big mess. Communication is a practiced, focused thing. But it's also often misunderstood, especially when it comes to sales. It's not about telling information to people, it's about having your customers tell things to you.

Here are two great strategies that you can use to improve your communication skills starting right now, today, this very minute.

Pay Attention: If it sounds redundant, it's to drive home the point that is one of the toughest things for most people to do. Focus 100% on the person who is talking to you. No wondering what you're going to have for lunch today. No itchy trigger finger on your smartphone hitting the refresh button on that eBay auction you've been following all weekend, no peeking over at your contemporaries to see how their own sales meetings/calls are going. There's no more important person in

SALES

the world right now than your customer. Make them believe that, by giving them your eye contact and your ears. Your attention makes the customer feel important. When they feel important, they gain trust and respect for you and are a whole lot more interested in trading your professionalism and knowledge for their hard-earned money. Listening does more than just let you hear their words. You can hear their tone, you can watch their body language, you can gauge just how important this decision is for them. Practice active listening around your office and around your home. Active listening entails eye contact, focus, and the ability to really hear what your customer is saying. When you're actively listening, it's easy to repeat what your client said, clarify any details, and ask relevant follow-up questions to keep the flow of information going. Body language is a great indicator of what the client thinks of you as well. If they're looking around your office instead of right at you, they're either bored or uninterested by what you are saying. If they have their arms folded across their chests, they are likely looking for ways out of the conversation and away from you. Your role model in this step should be the GPS system of your car. No, really. Think about it, you put a destination into the GPS and it starts leading you on the fastest route to get there. But when you eventually miss a turn, does the GPS scold you, shut down, or get upset? No. Because it is created with the idea that it must find out the best way to communicate with you. If you miss a left turn that will lead you to your destination, the GPS will recalculate the route and make the next best possible decision to get you back on course. Even if you miss 10 turns in a row, it keeps adjusting its communication style to fit yours. You have to emulate the GPS and do everything you can to understand your client's communication style in order to get the most out of them and help them the best way possible.

Use the Power of Storytelling. On any given day of the week, the kids of my friend can't seem to remember what happened in school that day, even though they just left there and were there for about 8-½ hours. These same children can recall with photographic precision however, the story of the time their father refused to eat his vegetables when he was six years old, and as a result was sent to bed early and not allowed to watch "Star Wars" on TV with his brother and father. Why are they so attuned to one memory but not to much more recent, relevant ones? It's the power of storytelling. Examples, anecdotes, and stories are some of the most powerful ways to communicate. It's a familiar process that we all have years and years of experience in. When someone starts telling a story, we listen in a little closer. We want to hear the setup, the execution, and the conclusion. Is it funny? Is it interesting? A tragedy? A lesson learned? We want to know. Customers can relate to stories, they can more easily understand things if they make a complex solution simple, and most importantly, they can remember them. You don't always have to use examples and stories in your communication, but they are often the perfect bridge from one idea to another. Make them as real as possible, although every great storyteller has some creative license for embellishment to make things more interesting. The best ones are those that make the unfamiliar become familiar, whether it's a different way of thinking, a different technology, or simply looking at an idea from a different perspective. Try to make them short and succinct. A 15-minute story about another customer is more likely to derail your message than enhance it. Remember, communication is a two-way street. Effective messages are not long messages. It's important to make sure you are just as attuned to receiving your customer's message.

Whether you are dealing with customers directly, organizing your contact list, or trying to decide who is worth pursuing and who is not, you've got to make decisions. Sales involves countless decisions on your part. You have to decide what questions to ask, what the best ways are to help customers, what products to offer, and so on. Making decisions it is not always easy and you are never guaranteed to make the right choice, but there are ways to strategize in order to have the best possible chance of success, as we will show here.

Get the Facts: Knowing the facts can be a huge step in the right direction. The facts should not be confused with your own opinion or someone else's ideas on the matter, they are just the facts. Many times, the facts can be hard to separate from opinions, especially our own. For example, say a customer leaves you a voicemail that they are interested in buying something. You've called them back four separate times and devoted lots of energy to those calls, but every time they opt out at the last minute without making a purchase. The conversations have been good but they won't seem to budge. When you're frustrated that you aren't getting anywhere with them, you might form the opinion that the person is a cheapskate who is wasting your time. That's just your emotions talking, however. Emotions are always present, and we all form opinions and ideas from them, but the facts are where our hearts must lie when we need to make big decisions.

Analyze information. Once you have all the facts gathered it's time to analyze. Think through every part of the decision you need to make, weigh the pros and cons, consider the needs of your customer versus the needs of your company, and determine your way forward. There might seem like no solutions and there might seem like many solutions. Write down everything to make the process easier. If it gets too complex, try some mind-mapping software.

Explore your options. In the example above, we're trying to decide if the customer is worth one more call with a direct sales pitch to see if they are interested or if we should cut bait. Exploring your options means approaching a problem from many different angles to determine a solution that fits best. Maybe we'd be better off sending the customer a newsletter now and then to let them decide when they're interested on their own. Or perhaps email them a coupon with a free gift offer provided they come into the store where we can speak to them one to one instead of over the phone. Having all the options laid out makes it infinitely easier to select the right one.

Pull the trigger: In other words, just make a decision. There's no guarantee it's the right decision, but more often than not it is better to make a less-than-perfect one than to not make one at all. You'll never move forward without making a decision, and moving forward is the only way to close a sale. Sales professionals make multiple big decisions every single day. Delaying those decisions can cost you valuable opportunities or make the problem that you need to solve become even worse. Being disciplined enough to engage in the decision-making process will ensure you make them quickly and efficiently. That can be the difference between a closed deal and a lost customer.

NOT PERSONALIZING YOUR MESSAGE IS THE BIGGEST MISTAKE YOU CAN MAKE WHILE SELLING TO ENTERPRISE CUSTOMERS.

Lacey Bell

CHAPTER 13

TAILOR YOUR APPROACH

We've talked about the power of MBS throughout this book and how your marketing and sales teams have to be aligned to give your company the best chance of success in the modern economy. Traditionally, marketing departments inform customers about a product, and sales team follow up with the selling of said product. When the two work together, they can accomplish amazing things such as guiding the customer through the journey like never before. The soft sell skills we learned about in the previous chapter apply to both business units here. Emulating the emotional connections that marketing departments make with potential customers will go a long way towards being able to do so yourself, with the results including long-term loyalty from customers and organic marketing as they spread the word on how impressive and honest a salesperson you are.

This leads us back to empathy, the essential ability to understand the emotional state and feelings of others. This is not to be confused with sympathy, where you give an emotional response to someone's conditions. Empathy means you can put yourself in their shoes, understand their points of strength and weaknesses, value what they have and appreciate what they want out of life, and then sell to them in a way that feels comfortable for them. That is the foundation for starting a professional relationship that will hopefully last long term and benefit both of you in the process.

So how do you develop empathy? The first step, and possibly the most important one, is to have a servant's heart.

To be empathetic, you must be willing to serve. You have to be genuinely interested in helping others get what they want before you are able to do likewise. For a salesman, that means focusing on your customer's needs long before you get around to considering your own quota. But being empathetic as a salesman is more than even that, it requires an extra step. You need to first focus on what your customer tells you is their pain point before you deliver your message about how you could improve their business.

Every customer is different, even if you sell in the same industry over and over again. Because of that, you must tailor your approach to fit every different situation. Develop the ability to be able to read what the customer needs in the moment and adjust your message, your tone, and your body language to respond in kind. If the customer is in a rush, look into that and give them the basics and the details, no fluff or small talk necessary. If they make it clear that they are in the initial stages of research for a solution, match their pace and make the conversation as much about them as it is about the product they are curious about. If you get the feeling that they are agitated sitting at your desk, get up and walk the showroom or the grounds with them. If they want to know what sets your company apart, give them a brief behind-the-scenes look at how the operation works. In short, use your powers of observation to see how you can catch their attention and get on the same wavelength as them. When the customer notices that you are willing to adjust to their needs, they'll see you're willing to be flexible to find the best possible solution for them. For a better look at this theory, let's dive into a couple of examples.

Our first scenario involves a past client showing up at the office unannounced. Our saleswoman, Katherine, quickly matches her tone of curiosity and smoothly transitions the conversation towards answering questions to get the necessary information on what she's interested in discussing.

Katherine: "Oh, pleasant surprise seeing you today, William, how are you?"

William: "I'm good! Just running errands and thought I'd pop in (laughs). You know, I was thinking about adding some work trucks to our fleet so I was kind of wondering about auto loans."

Katherine: "Okay, is there anything in particular you're wondering about?"

William: "Yeah, I want to know about those floating loans. My dad has a car rental business, and he buys his cars with one of those programs, so what's the benefit there?"

Katherine: "Well, I'd be happy to walk you through it."

Let's break that interchange down. William is clearly a former customer of Katherine's and feels comfortable enough with their relationship to swing by without an appointment in the middle of the day. He's interested in adding vehicles to his company's fleet. He could have done the research himself online or asked his dad about the process, but Katherine has established trust with him and so he reaches out. For her part, Katherine listens to his general ideas and then drills down to see if he has something specific in mind. Once he lays his cards on the table, she does not go after a sale, instead she's there to provide information to equip him to make the best possible decision.

In our next example, a customer wants to upgrade technology but knows he has very specific parameters for how much he has to spend. John steps in to clarify the information, but is largely satisfied to let the customer take the lead.

John: "So Vin, you said you're looking to upgrade some equipment at the factory?"

Vin: "Yes, I'm so excited, we finally get to upgrade our 3D printers. I feel like I've had the models I have now for ages. I'm so ready to get rid of them and come into the future.

John: "That is exciting! Any ideas on what you might like to buy?"

Vin: "Tons of ideas. So many things on my wish list. But I have a pretty good idea of what I can actually afford, and one thing's for sure, I'll be buying them on credit."

John: "Well you're in the right place. Let's see if we can figure out exactly what you'll need."

Notice how in each situation, John allowed the customer to define how fast they moved, what they talked about, and the direction the conversation took. In this second scenario, the customer is sharing news that he is clearly excited about as his company is making a long-needed upgrade. John might have just sold 50 3D printers to another customer this morning, but he tailors his energy level to Vin's enthusiasm and joins him in celebrating the big news. Vin does on to tell him two vital pieces of news: He has a budget he has to stick to and he wants to use a line of credit to pay for. That gives John two great parameters to work with and his mind is already in motion about things like: Does Vin's company already have a line of credit set up with John's company? How much is Vin's budget? What sort of bulk order deal can John create for Vin to give him a great price and terms of service? That is tailoring your approach. People feel comfortable with people who communicate like they do.

Another great way to build empathy is to validate your client or coworker's perspective. It's easy to listen to someone's story when you first meet them, say "OK", then proceed right into your standard sales pitch. But that does not help them, and in the long run does not help you either. Someone who feels you're just looking for a hard sell will have no problem walking away and buying their solution somewhere else; as we've mentioned many times, with the power of digital technology, a salesman is not a necessary part of most purchases anymore, merely an option. Validating a client's perspective lets them know that you clearly understand where they're coming from and can relate to what they are saying. This means being able to understand clients from every walk of life, every background, every geographic location, and every economic strata. Let's say you sell printing presses for a living to magazines, newspapers, and publishing companies. You do big sales routinely to well-established, well-funded clients who know your brand well. When a new customer contacts you from a fledgling printing company, its representative might let you know that money is an issue right now and they are really trying to find the best fit in terms of quality and affordability. A hard-selling salesman might look at this situation and just fire off his best pitch, realizing it's likely a one-time sale with little-to-no chance of repeat business. The soft-selling salesman does not just gloss over what he's heard, but takes the time to think what it feels like to be in the client's shoes, knowing that is a huge step forward in their business plan and they basically have one shot to get the best deal possible if that plan is to continue to the point where they start satisfying their own customers and turning a profit. For your big clients, this cost and decision are automatic. For a smaller company, this is the biggest decision they'll make this year, maybe even for several years. Really examine the attitude that you are projecting. You might be saying all the right things and following the necessary steps to make a sale, but does your attitude show that, or are you just providing the client with lip service? Faking interest does not just doom your success, it dooms that of your business as well. In everything you do when you're talking to a client, you're representing your company. If you're rude or condescending or bored or disrespectful, the customer will take that to mean that's how your company is as a whole. Be at your best every time you're with a client, and you'll have the best chance to make a great impression, start a new relationship, and have the best chance at converting a customer.

Finding the Balance between Hard and Soft Sales Skills

Everything in sales is a balance, from the opening discussion to the final price. We've focused a lot on soft sales skills in this chapter, but they are not the end of how to close a deal. Everything has to be balanced to where you are giving the client what they need while still being true to making the sale and being a valuable employee. You have to find that balance point between the technical, more concrete skills, and the softer, more relationship-oriented skills. In eras past, the hard skills were the ones that drove the train. But if you spend too much time on product knowledge and sales processes in the age of customization, the Internet, and digital technology, and you may very well lose a customer. On the flip side, if you spend too much time making friends with your customers, you might never close the actual sale. Understanding the fundamentals of the soft skills is an incredible first step, but they are just a part of the overall process. Being able to integrate them into your sales process is how you are going to go from decent sales person to exceptional sales person.

So, how do you know? How do you know when it's time to close the deal as opposed to talking about how your client's kids are doing in school? How do you know when it's time to bring out the big guns versus when it's time to ask them if they want an espresso? Clearly, there is no precise answer to this question, no solid rule. If there was, you wouldn't need this book or any other book, you'd just follow that one rule and laugh your way to the bank.

If anything, this is a time when you should trust your gut and let your analysis of the situation dictate which way to move next. No one likes to hear the answer "you'll just know", but that does tend to be the case once you become a seasoned sales professional. Clearly, not everyone is there yet, so to make things easier, here are some guidelines you can follow.

PERFORM A CUSTOMER ASSESSMENT

This is nothing more than what we've been talking about for the last few pages. Knowing who your customer is, how they tick, what they want, and how they like to be communicated with goes a long way towards determining whether soft, hard, or a mixture of your skills is necessary. For some customers business is simply business: They need a product, you have it. Tell them a price and let's get going. For that kind of customer you might never get past the soft skill of asking their name and how they're doing today. And that's perfect, that's the way that customer wants to conduct their business. You don't need to know their dog's name and what they had to eat last Tuesday. Give them the exact relationship they're seeking out and you'll never be wrong. Obviously, depending on the industry and who your target audience is, there will be other customers who are completely the opposite. They'll need lots of hand-holding as you walk them through the process from explaining how a system works to talking about various forms of payment to taking them through the product catalog to taking the time to discuss what they want, and what problem you can solve for them.

MAKE A PLAN

Once you've analyzed the customer and matched their personality and wants/needs to your list of skills, you can put a plan in place. This will give you a rough sketch of how you think the conversation is going to go and when you should use your hard skills and your soft skills. For instance, the first time you call on a customer, you may want to spend 20 minutes using your soft skills to understand how they communicate and build a relationship between you. If you're calling a customer who you've been dealing with for six months and who you have a great relationship with, you can chat for a few moments and then start with the hard skills like product knowledge to get the ball rolling towards your next sale.

ANALYZE YOUR RESULTS

If you make a plan, you need to see how it actually worked. After a conversation is complete, analyze how it went and how close to your plan things progressed. Write down what worked, what didn't, and what you need to do to make next time work more smoothly. Remember, this is always a work in progress and the more input you put in, the better the output will be. Weigh using your hard skills against your soft skills to find that balance you've been after.

YOU NEED TO BE ABLE TO PAINT
A PICTURE IN A CONVERSATION.
THE LOST PART OF SALES IS THE
STORYTELLING SIDE.

Richard Harris

CHAPTER 14

SALES STORYTELLING

We touched on storytelling in the previous chapter, but it really deserves its own space. Storytelling has previously been considered too long and drawn out of a process to be much help to sales, but as customers seek more individual attention, it becomes more and more key sales skill, not just something for marketers to employ to kick off a customer journey. What's the big change? Consider that when you are talking to a potential customer, you want to impart on them data and facts that will influence their final decision. We live in such a data-driven society that most people are going to lose interest in you if you stand there reciting numbers and statistics. How do you make data interesting? By crafting it into a story.

The purpose of a sales conversation is to gather information so that you solve a customer's problem or create an opportunity for them. Sharing information is far more effective if it is done in a narrative. People inherently connect with and remember stories better than they do simple facts and data. In fact, the London School of Business did a study on the difference between stories and standards presentations, and the results were off the charts. About 65-70% of people retained information they had acquired through listening to a story, but only 5-10% of those same people retained information shared through a presentation with data and statistics.

So if you want to be effective as a salesperson, and you want to be remembered, you need to learn to sell with a story.

Telling a story does not have to be as hard as you think, and truth be told you probably already have several in your memory bank that you can contour into the kind of narrative that can sell your product or service.

What are the keys to a great story?

For starters, it has to be true. OK, maybe not 100% true - it's a lot more fun if the bear that chased you and your friends was 8 feet tall instead of 5, or the car chase lasted for 3 hours instead of 1, but you get the general picture, you mostly need the facts to make it genuine. If it rings false in your head, it's not going to sound real on your lips. Stories need to be told from the heart, not your head. When a story is (mostly) true, you don't have to memorize it; you could tell it today and tomorrow, then not for three months, and still remember all the cadences. The more you believe it, the more your customer will too.

Of course, telling a story just to tell a story doesn't move the needle a lot on your relationship with the customer or with their journey. Make sure the story is relevant to what you're trying to accomplish and that the customer can not only relate to it, but draw connections from their situation to what's going on in the tale without you having to hold their hand and guide them down the path.

Great stories need to engage the customer as well. You want them to get involved and feel some sort of connection to the protagonist, whether it's fear, shame, disgust, kinship, whatever. Kick the story off with phrases like "I'm sure you know someone like this" or "Remember the time when" to get them feeling connected.

Make your story detailed so that the customer can see it in their mind's eye. You didn't meet your wife at a restaurant, you met her at that Italian place down on Sixth Street that has the original pipe organ and those incredible breadsticks. When the client asks you about the wildest order you've ever taken, you don't say it was a few years ago and the client bought 20 or 30 limousines for a musician's party that night, you tell them that it was June 7, 2009, you had just sat down at your desk when you got a call from a guy claiming to be Mick Jagger's tour manager asking to rent 35 white stretch limos for a party Mick had decided to throw that night. Make the connection by having the story directly late to the customer and the sale at hand.

Here's a great example of how storytelling can augment sales. Paul is just sitting down with his client Mara.

Paul: "Well Mara, again, thank you for making time with me today."

Mara: "Yeah, of course, I'm really excited to find out what sort of software you have for our business office. We are already nearing the end of construction, so time is running short, but I know we are in the right hands, especially since you helped me and my sister with her company's needs."

Paul: "It is my pleasure, and yes, I think I have something you will like. I know you have some time constraints today, so let's just jump right into it. Here's the software package I selected for you based on the contract you sent over and what we discussed on the phone."

Mara: "Okay, (sighs) oh this looks great. You can't beat this price. Now, I want to say yes to this, but my one reservation is, if I sign with a big company like you guys, I feel like I'm going to get lost in the shuffle and get passed on to a third-party vendor. Is that how it works here?"

Paul: "It's a good question. There are third-party techs we use when we install software. But I always like to use your sister Debbie's business as an example of how we are different than most companies. She needed that stuff installed and her staff up to speed in about a week. We don't trust anyone but ourselves for a job like that. My team was out there from Day One to get our hands dirty solving all their problems on site. I gave her my personal cell and promised that I would get back to her at the end of the day if she needed me. And I upheld that promise, just ask her. "

Mara: "I do remember her telling me that and you guys really came through for her."

Paul: "Yes, ma'am, so to sum it up, we can absolutely do the same thing for you. I'll make myself available on my cell and that way, you are comfortable the whole way through.

Mara: "All right then. Let's do this!"

Rather than just answer the question, Paul used a story that was both highly relevant to Mara and detailed and engaging. Plus, he concluded by making the connection to Mara's situation crystal clear.

That's the essential power of storytelling. It draws a picture for your customers, and helps them understand and remember how what you're selling benefits them and their business.

PRESENTING TO YOUR PROSPECT

Presenting is the single biggest event that determines if the sale has any potential of closing. After doing some initial qualification, you finally have your prospects in a place where they're receptive to being educated, convinced, persuaded, and motivated to purchase your product or service offerings.

This is where the spotlight is on you and it's your chance to shine, to show your prospects your knowledge of your company, your product, your competitive advantage, and to demonstrate what you've learned about them.

You have a captive audience waiting to be convinced. Most business presentations are delivered virtually from a desktop through a web collaboration or web conferencing tool. They take place after the initial qualification, where you have identified there's a potential opportunity and you have a good idea of their needs. This happens somewhere between the second to the fifth call.

Business presentations must be short, no more than 15 minutes in length, and must be delivered in plain language. This is not the time for a lot of buzzwords or jargon. These must be as short, around the 15 minute time range, and not a product or technical data dump. It's important to create a presentation that showcases your product or service, that emphasizes your confidence in it, that speaks to your prospect's needs, that does not waste their time and holds their interest in a compelling way that moves the deal to a close.

When customizing your presentation for your prospects, get to know who you will be presenting to, what their backgrounds are, what they're looking for, and what they expect. Put yourself in their shoes, and think about what's running through their minds when they're watching your presentation. This is where your empathy kicks in and you are able to understand the customer at a much deeper level than before. They may be thinking:

"Why should I buy your product?

"What problems will it solve?"

"What type of short or long-term return will it give me?"

"What if I don't buy now?"

"What will it do for my business?"

"How will it help me reach my goals?"

Remember that your presentation happens after some initial qualification takes place. That means that you're not emulating a cold call with this presentation, you're trying to evolve your relationship with the customer. Introduce yourself, then state your objective. Make sure you include any needs you've uncovered in addition to addressing any concerns that the client had during your initial information-gathering phase. Ask if there's anything you might have left out, or if the points you've made are valid. Make sure you keep the presentation running smoothly without big lags in time or periods of quiet. Ask if you can schedule a demo. Keep them talking and thinking until it's time to make a decision.

HOW TO HANDLE OBJECTIONS

Sales are not going to go smoothly. There are always going to be rough waters when you try to bring a ship safely into port. Sometimes it will be one big swell that you are able to ride out, other times it will be one breaker after another that leave you feeling like you've been ambushed by a tidal wave of objections.

Don't be discouraged. Objections just mean that there are hidden needs that need solving. And although sales changed dramatically in the last couple of decades, objections have not. They still fall into the same five main categories that they have for decades.

Once you understand these categories, you'll have a better idea of how you can rebound from them. The objection categories include:

Need
Relationship
Authority
Product/service
Price

Let's look at some of these categories more closely. Occasionally, a customer's need has decreased since the last time they spoke with you. Markets change, sometimes overnight. The urgency and the need for your solution may easily take a back seat. Objections may sound something like this:

"Nah, we're not interested."

"We're not ready to do anything right now."

This type of objection usually happens early in the call and comes up because you haven't communicated any value on your solution. You have to convince the client that what you are offering is essential to solving their problems immediately and that they can't find it anywhere else. Let's face it, if the client was not interested or not ready to make a move on a purchase at this point, they never would have come to the presentation in the first place. Companies' time is too valuable to sit through a sales presentation they have no interest in. When this sort of response comes up, counter by asking them questions like "What exactly are you looking for?" and "What variables are keeping you from making a decision right now?" Probe them for information to see where your presentation is lacking.

The second category is relationship. People do business with people they like. Your customer may be resisting simply because something went wrong with your relationship in the past or they're heavily committed to the competition. You might hear objections that sound like this.

"We're very happy with our current vendor."

"We've had a bad experience with your company in the past."

The reason they'll respond like this is that you haven't established enough trust or a relationship with them for them to understand how you compare with the competition. Your soft skills need to be on display here to let the customer see that you are a figure to be trusted and that your opinion is as good as gold. This is another case where you aren't hearing the whole story in their response and you need to dig deeper for it.

Think about it: If you were completely happy with a vendor, why would you take a call from another one and come as far as to participate in a presentation. If you are 100% satisfied with where your kids go to school, you don't go touring a new private school just for the heck of it. Whether it's conscious or subconscious, there's something lacking in your current solution that you are looking for. That's what you have to find in your customers.

The third category is authority. With more decision-makers involved in the process, there are more "no-pos" popping up every day. No-pos have no power and no authority to make purchase decisions. Your prospect may not be that power buyer. When you determined from your decision-making status in your information gathering, you should also identify the lead decision-maker. Objections you might hear will sound like this.

"Just send me your information and if someone is interested, we'll get back to you."

" I can't get the higher level to approve of this project."

What you need to do when you get this type of objection is start calling around and learn the chain of command at your client's business. Move away from your contact, who may be holding you back or down. This can be a delicate process, so remember to really mix your soft skills in here. The person you've built the relationship with cannot get you where you want to go, but they still likely exude some control over the person. Figure out the exact relationship between the person you know and the person you want to know, and if one can get you closer to the second.

The fourth area is your product and service. And although customers know more than ever before, they have less patience with anything too complicated that lacks scalability and integration. Your solution might have a steep learning curve and cannot be implemented as easily. So the objections you might hear might sound like this.

"Your service offerings are way too complicated for us."

"This is overkill for what we need. We have a very small network."

When you hear this, you need to move into educating them about your product or service and neutralize their fears of trying something new. Change can be a tough thing for people to get on board with. On many occasions it has to be a slam dunk that what you're offering them is a no-brainer.

And the last category is price. Not everyone can afford to buy what they truly need. That's why it's so important to qualify your prospects. If you thoroughly gather information on their budget and their price range, you'll be able to tell the difference between whether the problem is really price or not. Saying price is the barrier is usually the easiest way out. Dig a little deeper with questions designed to expose the underlying causes of that answer and see what you can find. So objections you might hear will sound like this:

"Your product is way too expensive and we're very small."

" We can't make any purchases on new investments."

The price objection is the most popular objection, but research shows that it's actually the least-popular reason why prospects reject your solution. Spend more time creating value and less time talking about budget. It's time to dig deeper to understand the objections you receive. Especially chase after those lost deals to understand what went wrong.

CLOSING THE SALES

Closing is the time where all your sales skills pay off, both hard and soft. Building a healthy sales process is essential to closing sales, but in the end the salespeople must understand when is time to ask for closing. This is a make-or-break moment in sales. Choosing the right phrases to seal a sales deal is crucial. The traditional sales closing techniques usually employ some psychological tricks designed to give that final nudge, like highlight the scarcity or summarizing the previously agreed-points and package everything with a reasonable latest discount.

These closing techniques probably seem a little old-fashioned, and maybe they doesn't match with all the work done previously in the sales process that you put in place, with the result that they make you come across as pushy and self-serving, which isn't the best impression to give when kicking off a business partnership.

A more modern sales closing technique, could be a question or series of questions. In fact, when you discovered the customer needs and effectively shared how your product or service is a specific satisfactory solution and you addressed all the objections, it is the time to ask them for closing. Here some example:

"Are there any reasons why we can't proceed?". This question asks either for closure or more information as to why the customer isn't quite convinced. It's win-win.

"It seems like [product/service] is a good fit for [company]. What do you think?" Because you end by asking for their opinion automatically makes your prospect think of all the reasons they're interested in buying and it sounds very genuine.

"Why don't you give it/us a try?" This sound very simple but doing this you are downplay the risk from "commitment" to "chance" leveraging the rapport that you built with the soft skills.

"Ready to move forward? I can send over the contract right now." Everyone likes the idea of progress. Your prospects will be likelier to commit if they associate the purchase with forward momentum.

Like you can see there are many approach as a sales you can take, you can also be more technical setting customer expectations, for example:

"If we implement by X date, I estimate you can start seeing ROI by August. That means we'd need to close by X date. Is that enough time for you to make a decision?".

Being skilled at closing is arguably one of the most important techniques a salesperson can master, so elaborate your closing technique to match the narrative of your sale process.

SECTION THREE: ALIGNMENT

IF AN OPPORTUNITY ISN'T EFFECTIVELY QUALIFIED, THE SALES REP WILL OPERATE UNDER THE MISTAKEN IMPRESSION THAT THE DEAL IS THEIRS TO WIN.

Dave Stein

CHAPTER 15

WHY RUNNING SEPARATE SALES & MARKETING TEAMS IS FAILING YOU

Marketing is your cost center and sales is your profit center. Heard that one before? Or some variation of it? We're not surprised. When I look at this statement, it seems generic but also contains some truth to it. Over the years, I've seen plenty of marketers, but only a few can sell in an environment that casts sales as the commercial lifeblood for companies.

The thing is, sales is a tough gig. Not everyone is cut out for it. Over the years, I've developed a deeper respect for salespeople than for marketers because sales teams live out there on the front line in a world full of No, Not Now, and No Thanks.

They don't have the luxury of hiding behind the confines of a desk at the head office. Sales teams are out there having to dust themselves off day in, day out as they head to their next appointment with renewed enthusiasm despite being beaten down by their last stop.

Without a strong lead-generating machine behind them, sales is a lonely place. If they're not getting the support they need, it's likely they won't be interested when there's an employee conference and the marketing manager is presenting enthusiastically on their latest social media efforts. The problem is the worst marketers mistake output for outcomes when all that matters are the things they can do to help their sales teams get results. Marketers yearn for respect from their sales peers, yet do nothing to earn it. Creating strategies, making plans or making customer journeys are not an outcome, sales are. Yet when sales and marketing are siloed, there is little either can do to break out of that mold and being helping each other improve both of their positions. The responsibility has to come from above, in the C-suite level of executives whose job it is to break out of the traditional shackles of standard corporate practice and find new ways to innovate in the changing digital environment.

There are many compelling arguments for centralized versus decentralized models when it comes to how best to manage sales and marketing departments, but in my experience the best company performance I've seen is when sales and marketing are aligned and led under the same manager or general manager.

The cons of a decentralized sales and marketing model are:

- Silos and patch protection
- Politics
- Distrust
- Miscommunication
- Lack of information flow and market insights

The pros of a centralized sales and marketing model are:

- Greater efficiencies
- Increased efficacy
- Less distraction and business interruption
- Greater teamwork and cultural strength
- Less reporting lines
- Less "BS"

Being aligned and responsible for common, shared objectives means less company energy and resources are being depleted. This energy can be better directed outside into the market where it is needed most to attract and convert new customers, and instill loyalty into them to act as your word-of-mouth organic advertising to do the same to others. The sooner the sales and marketing departments are merged, the sooner you will begin reaping the benefits while easing the inter-department pain and frustrations that have long existed.

The alignment described here isn't a new concept. Sales and marketing in the past have worked hand in hand as one close knit team. We see it all the time in startups where constant coordination and communications are necessary to get a business past that nascent stage and off the ground. At that point, everyone in-house is focused on sales because it is their absolute life blood. However, as businesses grow and incomes increase, businesses become more complex. That's when companies think they need to create two separate departments because it will allow each of them to have a greater focus - one charged with generating leads (marketing) and one dedicated with closing them (sales). And this, as the classic novel tells us, is where everything falls apart.

The very thing that served them so well in their early days is the thing they now decide to change. Just because you couldn't justify separate sales and marketing departments when you were small, doesn't mean you can justify it now just because you're big. What worked well then can continue to work well now. It astounds me when businesses create more complexity, especially when the model of simplicity is already working well enough. It's counterproductive and completely unnecessary.

The problem I see too often with separate sales and marketing teams is that business owners are tearing their hair out like parents with kids who continually fight. It ends up with the unenviable "them and us" situation. Due to a lack of common understanding, the cracks begin to show and without the right management, valuable sales opportunities are lost between the two. As sales revenue drop, the predictable blame game starts with companies ending up being busier doing business with themselves than they should be with their customers. The refereeing becomes a business distraction and they lose their focus looking inward instead of outward. And while they're doing that, their competitors are swooping in to pry away old customers and round up new ones.

The challenge with a centralized sales and marketing function is that it demands talented employees who are highly qualified in both disciplines.

Finding good salespeople is hard enough. But you can double the pressure when it comes to finding a seasoned Sales & Marketing Manager/GM. I meet very few marketers who are comfortable being managed by metrics or hard data. Many prefer to hide behind the softer measures of success like brand consideration or awareness.

They like to leave the harder stuff to the salesmen and saleswomen. When it comes to sales teams, they often have little regard and respect for the brands they represent and don't understand how important marketing is to build a differentiated brand that justifies a premium. Their commercial arrangement and need for targets, bonuses or commissions can run counter to brand values or positioning (the softer but still important stuff). Results are all that matters to them, and the ends justify the means even if it means sacrificing margin. It's hard to argue against results because numbers are what we use to measure business performance. However, if short-term sales are being achieved at the expense of longer-term brand positioning or customer experience, it's a short game that might work for a while but will eventually fizzle out.

So how do you solve this problem? Sometimes you find talent that can be coached to develop dual competencies but those people are rare, and usually in such high demand that they don't stay around very long. I find it easier to start with sales talent and help them develop broader marketing competencies because sales are a commercial necessity that you must prioritize. Or you can structure a leadership team that has a stand-out sales captain supported by very good marketing lieutenants. That leadership can make it work. The leader needs to demonstrate evidence and understanding of a broader perspective by being able to respect and support both sales and marketing contribution to company success. Getting everyone to play on the same team can be tough right away, so make sure that you have team-building exercises, a closer look at everyone's duties as they apply to the big picture, and ample opportunities to mingle and get to know each other in non-work environments.

The efficiencies of management, reduced costs, greater productivity, better alignment and speed to market make for a good business case by themselves. But for the magic to really happen, much like the best sports teams, you need to create the right environment. One where there is a mutual respect for each other's area of expertise, real and sometimes brutal honesty, continuous feedback loops, genuine inter-dependency, and an uninterrupted journey between lead generation and sales conversion. In this environment, knowledge sharing and front-line intel flows unimpeded so that any customer or competitor insights can be actioned quickly and efficiently to take advantage of a market opportunity.

So if you want to win a bigger market share, I recommend you look at how you can merge your sales and marketing departments into one efficient centralized team. You can use this combined energy and talent to beat the competition together rather than struggle separately.

When you create that alignment, you'll be a powerful force better equipped to focus on what's most important out there: winning.

The gap between marketing and sales teams has been around since the two functions were created and is usually just accepted as an irreparable inconvenience in many businesses. What are some of their general differences that make it such a difficult environment for both to coexist?

Sales thinks only they are worried about the current quarter while marketing thinks they are the only ones who are thinking strategically.

Sales wonders why they have to generate all their own leads while marketing complains that sales ignores or criticizes everything they generate.

Sales thinks marketing is lightweight and easy while marketing thinks salespeople will say anything to get a deal.

It is time for this fighting to stop.

As the spread of the Internet, digital technology, and social media transform the B2B buying process, aligning the different departments has never been more critical to driving revenue and growth.

The lack of alignment between sales and marketing is causing businesses across the globe to fail every year. So much so that misalignment is costing businesses more than a $1 trillion per year. That's right, $1 trillion (with 12 zeros).

In fact, sales and marketing misalignment is the number one reason why an organization's annual revenue stagnates or, worse, declines.

This issue has become such a hot topic that companies have started listing their marketing priorities ahead of understanding marketing ROI and reducing acquisition costs.

If this sounds familiar, then now is the time to address the sales and marketing alignment challenge. Because if you don't, your business is unlikely to grow any further. So, how do you successfully align both teams? The answer is blending, which means together seamlessly to close more sales.

When sales and marketing are combined, it becomes far easier to track results and make high-impact changes with the final goal of increasing your customer base. Even better, with strong analytics, a lot of those decisions can be made close to "real time".

ALIGNMENT

THE CONS OF A DECENTRALISED
SALES AND MARKETING MODEL ARE:

THE PROS OF A CENTRALISED SALES
AND MARKETING MODEL ARE:

SILOS AND PATCH
PROTECTION

POLITICS

GREATER
EFFICIENCIES

INCREASE
EFFICACY

DISTRUST

MISCOMMUNICATION

LESS DISTRACTION
AND BUSINESS
INTERRUPTION

GREATER
TEAMWORK AND
CULTURAL
STRENGTH

LACK OF
INFORMATION
FLOW AND
MARKET INSIGHT

LESS REPORTING
LINES

AS MARKETING CONVERGES
WITH CUSTOMER SERVICE AND
SALES, MARKETING TODAY IS
MORE ABOUT HELPING AND LESS
ABOUT HYPING.

Joel Book

CHAPTER 16

THE EVOLUTION OF SALES AND MARKETING

Gone are the old days of the "ABC – always be closing" approach to sales and using cold call "spray and pray" techniques to find new prospects.

Today, sales is part of the wider marketing mix, and marketing is directly accountable in sales process.

The reason for this change is because consumer habits have evolved, and the old sales techniques no longer work. Due to the introduction of sales automation tools (CRM) and marketing software, you're now able to collect a wide range of data on prospects, making the whole process more data driven.

So the question is: How to align sales and marketing in your business?

There are 8 clear steps to get where you want to go:

1.   Restructure the customer journey, starting from the awareness stage at the beginning, right down through to the brand loyalty stage. Everything should be tied together as a single, flexible experience. Use omni-channel marketing to ensure this process is cohesive; that is, every touchpoint along the customer journey is telling the same message in the same voice - be it your company website, advertising, social media, etc. Depending on your business, this can include smart sensors in your brick-and-mortar store that "read" how far into the location a customer travels and what items they interact with. You can also use heat charts and other online analysis to get the same results from your company website.

2.   Develop an agreed-upon target customer persona in order to get everyone on the same page and be more effective as a team. You will need to help sales and marketing agree on a customer profile by creating an ideal customer persona document together. Compiling customer personas has never been more accurate than now thanks to the AI subset practice of Machine Learning (ML). It can process data far quicker than any human ever could and notice patterns that would take us years or maybe never to notice, then collate them into actionable analysis.

3. Use a "marketing first" approach. This means that marketers find (or target) potential customers who have a specific problem and show them how it can be solved. The marketing department warms up and nurtures new leads by sharing information on the product and selling the features and benefits. The age of digital technology has sent marketing from an era of guesswork to an era of knowledge. Analysing search terms on Google and developing keywords gives marketers unprecedented insight into what customers want. Engage them on social media and in other 1-to-1 conversations to drill down to the specifics of what they are looking for in your industry.

4. Measure joint key performance indicators (KPIs), so your team is uniting under one common goal, not only with hard metrics, but also with the softer ones. Eventually, we aim for a world where there are no marketing goals nor sales goals, just customer goals that both units work in harmony to achieve. It won't happen overnight but eventually the two units will realize they are two sides of the same coin that work together to achieve business success.

5. Gather sales feedback. This is one of the most powerful things that you can do after you align both teams. Look at the feedback you get directly from your customers, also known as Voice of Customer (VOC) data. This is another area where digital technology allows us to do so much more than our predecessors even 20 years ago. Not only is the Internet flush with sites that allow customers to review pretty much every

product under the sun, but we have multiple ways to follow up with customers beyond the simple cold call a few days later. Be innovative and use social media, email, text messages, etc. to gather information on the sales process and the customer experience. These are the two most vital components necessary to improve how you engage with your customers.

6. Keep marketing messages consistent. Some 21% of B2B marketers cite "giving the customer a poor impression of our organization" as one of the most detrimental factors resulting from poor content marketing and sales alignment. This is another reason why sales and marketing should work under one roof. Getting the customer excited and intrigued about a product needs to carry over into the process of convincing them to buy it. This tracks back to the omnichannel marketing technique we spoke of earlier. Everything that the marketing department generates centers on one or two central themes that drive brand awareness and deliver key points to customers that sales staff then expands on in creating the perfect sales solution.

7. Create marketing-led sales assets. One of the most popular B2B marketing strategies used today is content marketing. When used by both sales and marketing teams, content marketing is highly effective at nurturing prospects through the different stages of the sales lifecycle. Content marketing refers to anything outside of traditional marketing that your company uses to attract interest. Blogs, articles, infographics, white papers, webinars, the list can be as big as

your staff is creative. In offering multiple forms of content, you will cast a wider net that allows you to connect with different types of customers who put value into different forms of content, and help them start or continue their customer journey.

8. Work together in post-sale retention and growth. There's a lot more to gain from this alignment, especially if the teams work together in order to grow and retain customers. One of the first things every business person learns early on is that it is a lot easier to keep a customer than to establish a new one. Salespeople are perpetually busy (hopefully) and following up with customers who just walked out the door can be tough when there's another batch right behind them that they're looking to close. Automation tools can come into play here: Tasks can be created to follow up with customers via text after three days, email after a week, and a phone call after a month, keeping your company fresh in their minds without eating up existing man-hours to do so. You can generate recurrent sales and not miss on profits you should be making from existing customers.

NO ONE CAN WHISTLE A SYMPHONY. IT TAKES A WHOLE ORCHESTRA TO PLAY IT.

H.E. Luccock

CHAPTER 17

DEPARTMENT COLLABORATION

It's never easy when you start meshing two departments together into a single unit, even more so when it involves two entities that are 1) generally autonomous outside of reporting to the board of directors and 2) used to getting their way all the time.

No to say that it's not worth it to try. According to the Harvard Business Review, proper alignment between sales and marketing leads to 32% higher revenue, 38% higher win rates, 36% more retaining customers, 24% faster growth rates, and 27% faster revenue growth. Those numbers are way too big and too frequent to be thought of as flukes. The same report says that businesses in the US are costing themselves $1 trillion yearly based on this misalignment.

The best way forward when you're getting sales and marketing together is to make it as transparent a process as possible, which means treating everyone like an adult and giving them a timeline of what's going to happen, why it's going to happen, and perhaps most importantly the positives that will result from a willing harmony of team members from both sales and marketing. Change is inevitable in any occupation, and none more so that those so affected by the coming of the Internet and the digital age.

The first step should be an initial meeting that involves everyone in both departments and their superiors among the C-suite level of employees. While that roster of attendees probably doesn't sound like it can be laid back, you still need to find a way to keep the meeting casual. Some ideas about that are to have it off-site or on a casual Friday where people can dress down from their business clothes to more of bluejeans and sneakers feel. Including a lunch or some other casual meal. This should not be a step-by-step grind-it-out meeting in which every single detail of the merge is revealed and everyone's questions come spilling out. This is a meeting to get everyone excited about the possibilities. Better synergy between sales and marketing means less doubling up on certain processes, more sales, and better profits, which generally translate into higher sales commissions, more pay raises, and better bonuses. Explain what your company is trying to achieve and answer the more basic of questions. It's a big change, and there is a large segment of the population that fears change and would much rather have everything stay the same from the day they are hired until the day they retire.

In addition to announcing the merge, there are three great topics to talk about at the first meeting.

They are:

Points of friction in your sales cycle

What the ideal lead looks like

Who your customer personas are

When you're discussing the point of friction in your sales cycle, you can ask each team to describe the process - break them into teams or have them do it at different tables. Once they've taken 10-15 minutes to come up with their sales cycle then see how they match up. If there are discrepancies, discuss why. Once those have been discussed and agreed upon, make a point of establishing a final version of the sales process and make sure everyone understands their role in it and what stages marketing and sales are responsible for.

Once that is done, circle back around to talk about the rough spots, the friction points. Which parts aren't working as well as they could or as well as they should? This will be a part where they might be some finger-pointing between departments, but the key is to keep everyone talking about their own team and its experience with the sales cycle. The problem might well be something from the other department, but the goal is to look at things objectively. It is very likely that both sides will have a lot to say, but the idea is that getting all those problems out in the open is the way to start working on solutions to them.

Once everyone has had their say, you need to move on to what the collaboration is all about: closing deals. This is the ultimate goal of every single member of both departments, and their synergy is what is going to move your company to that next level of success, where it stops being marketing and sales bumping into each other. No more doing the same job twice with only half of the expected result. By spelling out everyone's roll and using the following checklist to iron out the rough spots, you will see your new-look company move rapidly from stumbling along like a newborn deer to sprinting across the sales environment like a cheetah, outdistancing the competition and moving in for the kill time after time.

Here's a few tips to keep everything running smoothly during the transition:

SALES SHARES PROSPECT QUESTIONS ALONG THE CUSTOMER JOURNEY

In this first solution, you can already see the power of collaboration as your sales people solve one of the most vexing problems that marketers have: What do our customers and potential customers want to know about? It's something that marketers throw everything including the kitchen sink at when they are striving to create their plans, doing all sorts of research from SEO to social media and all points in between seeking to know what specifically their customers pain points are and what information they are looking for when they start the customer journey. And then there are their new sales coworkers who talk to said customers literally every single day and can provide those answers almost effortlessly. The endless toils of one business unit rendered null and void by the other. It's a bit like marketing has been trying to start a fire on a deserted island all these years, and suddenly sales landed in yacht stuffed to the brim with matches and lighter fluid. By using the customers they already have as a sounding board, marketers are now able to turn those questions into executable plans to start pull other customers from other lines of communications. In our long-standing example of PawTastic Pup Treats, customers might be asking about another dog treat company who was forced to issue a massive recall due to toxic ingredients. The customers are concerned about the ingredients but don't have much information about it or what it can do. That sort of invaluable information is handed off from sales to marketing, which then creates a strategy of blogs, videos, and a whitepaper explaining what the toxic chemical is, what its effect is on dogs, and why PawTastic Pup Treats only uses all-natural ingredients instead of this type of chemical in all of its products.

ASK MARKETING REPS TO SHARE THEIR BUYER PERSONAS WITH SALES

First you get something, then you give something. This is not something most marketing professionals are willing to just idly hand over, so this needs to be framed in just the right manner. Buyer personas are the lifeblood of everything that marketing departments do, the foundation for how they craft their strategies and long-term plans. Asking for their buyer persona information casually is a bit like asking Colonel Sanders what makes Kentucky Fried Chicken so tasty. You're asking to pull back the curtain and see what makes the Wizard of Oz so great and powerful. These personas are the result of lots of research from age and gender to position in a company, favorite TV shows, and pain points in the sales process. A big part of that is language - not like English or Chinese, but the kind of language that the person speaks when they are talking about the problems they need solved. Are they technical? Are they price-related? Is it about Product A vs. Product B? Do they value trust and long-time commitment? Finding that out is a huge step forward for how the sales team will approach them.

BREAK DOWN WHY MARKETING LEADS AREN'T WORKING

This is the part of the collaboration that Tyrion Lannister would call "walking on rotten ice". Press down too hard and it shatters whatever you've built so far. Most of us are OK with a critique from a supervisor, but when it comes from someone on our own level but outside the department, it can be a pressure point. If what marketing is generating as quality leads are not turning out that way, the sales team must address it with them because it doesn't let either side do their job right. It can't be straight criticism, however, this is a joint effort, and pointing fingers breaks down community real quick. A better strategy is to bring examples of quality leads that have converted and why they converted, then compare those to some of the examples that aren't making the grade. When some common ground can be found, a lead scoring system can be developed that works for both departments. Such a system could be reviewed, tweaked, and updated on a regular basis to ensure it is working properly.

WHAT MAKES A GOOD LEAD?

We're living in one of the most eventful times of change in sales history. The dawn of Big Data, Artificial Intelligence, and Machine Learning has altered a lot about how sales leads are built and sent out into the world. The old guard of sales has a hard time letting go from the "gut feeling" process of reading faces and voices that they cut their teeth on 25 years ago and have used successfully ever since. The reality is that a lot of these salespeople don't complain about the new technology, they just don't use it. Marketing qualified leads don't stand a chance against their ability to shoot the breeze about life, the universe, and everything with a customer and eventually get a deal done. These are people that will need extra convincing on the synergy, mostly in real hard figures, not just straight data.

MQLS HAVE A HABIT OF CHANGING

The perfect MQL from a year ago might be nothing of the sort next Tuesday. Dynamics change in the world of sales leads all the time, but it wasn't until we started using Big Data and analysis that we were aware how quickly they changed or had the power to do something about it. Today's consumer is quite fickle, particularly given their ability to switch from one product to another in the blink of an eye and click of the mouse. The definition of an MQL for each company depends on what the product is, what the offer defines it as, and what the customer's current pain points are. Sales and marketing both have to change with these transformative answers. They have to be aware of outside forces like global economics, unemployment, natural disasters, and more. Sometimes a new product will shift your audience, sometimes new technology will shift your price point, all research must be done to keep up.

TEAM UP TO REFINE LEAD GENERATION FORM FIELDS

There is a better-than-average chance that an IT person put together the form for your lead generation and slapped the information that either your head of marketing or head of sales gave them for the forms. That might have been convenient for the time and effort required to get the ball rolling, but if we've learned one thing in this process, it's that language counts. The language you specifically want in that forms versus what someone from IT might put there could be the gap the size of an ocean. Sales and Marketing must work together to create the fields of your lead generation forms, understanding the lead generation process from start to finish, in this way they can begin to identify any bottlenecks that could hold your company back from success.

IF LEADS DON'T WORK, DUMP THEM

This isn't the 1960s when leads were all direct mail and phone calls. If the ones you have aren't working out for you, you need to cut the cord. Things happen close to real-time in lead generation, and if you're not getting bites on some of yours, it's time to cut bait and move on. This means keeping the data in your CRM up to date. Businesses open and close, people leave positions and take new ones, it's the business cycle, and you need to keep up with it. If a lead is going nowhere after a few months, dump it.

DEVELOP THOUGHT LEADERS

Your target customers are going to see a ton of salespeople over the course of a day, a week, a month. That's a lot of annoying phone calls, canned emails, and the same old "have I got a deal for you" conversations. Every salesperson tries to set themselves apart, but when you have a marketing department tied to your sales staff, you have the rare opportunity to do in-house promotion that not only makes your sales people more well known, but can transform them into thought leaders who will gain the ear of your potential customers who will start looking to them not only for products and services, but also for insight into important industry issues. Find out what issues your sales staff is passionate about and what issues they are knowledgeable about. Promote them in your content - have them write blogs or have them ghostwritten for them. Have them star in videos. Make them THE person to follow on Twitter, Facebook, and LinkedIn when it comes to the market your company is in. By the time a customer meets the salesperson face to face, it should give them the feeling of meeting an industry rock star.

SHARING DATA MAKES EVERYONE SMARTER

The more data you have to make decisions with, the more well-informed those decisions can be. Customers are smarter than ever and have just as many opportunities to do research online as you do. You're not going to find many pushovers among them. That means that they're expecting the "how you doing?" email after three days and the "Just checking in" text after seven. If you're going to hold their attention and maneuver them down the sales cycle, you're going to have to deliver real value to them when you make contact. Otherwise, you're just another candidate for the SPAM folder. Use data collected at both ends to offer really premium content to your potential customers. Let sales deliver info on case studies that tell the tale of interesting customers who used your product and have made great strides since. Find really compelling stats and build infographics from there. The possibilities are really limited and this is where the creative spark can shine.

GIVE THE STRAGGLERS TO MARKETING

Some potential customers just aren't ready to buy, and that's OK but you shouldn't waste one extra second for your sales staff's time on them once they've been determined to not be on the track for a sale. Once that determination has been made, make the very subtle transition of the customer's file back to your marketing team. They can plug in to the customer along the sales journey and determine where they are along the customer journey and begin taking them step by step down the path until they are back in a position where they are ready to buy, that frees up sales to go after the big fish.

Do it Right, Customers for Life.

One of the first lesson every person learns is that it's infinitely easier to keep an existing customer than acquire a new one. That means you don't just shake hands and walk away when the bill is paid, you nurture that relationship by letting each side do what it does best. Marketing can develop collateral custom designed to keep satisfied customers coming back for more while sales keeps applying the personal touch with customized offers and checkups.

LET THE MARKETERS MARKET

Many customers are not impressed with sales talk, in fact it often makes them shy away from making a purchase. One of the jobs of marketing teams is to write the content that doesn't come across as a hard sale. There's a lot of nuance and tone there, and it might sound like a foreign language to sales staff members, but it's kind of supposed to. It's sort of like playing beach volleyball together, marketing sets up the assist and sales knocks down the kill. When the two sides talk over each other is when things get uncomfortable. Trust the other side to deliver or you'll find the decline hits you both.

Talk to each other, all the time.

The more you talk to one another, the more you'll understand each other, get the point of each other's work, speak each other's language, and have each other's backs. This synergy cannot be taught or bought, it can only be experienced. Once you've got a mutual understanding and can start putting out the little fires before they turn into big flames, things will start to go a lot more smoothly.

YOU HAVE TO GENERATE REVENUE AS EFFICIENTLY AS POSSIBLE. AND TO DO THAT, YOU MUST CREATE A DATA-DRIVEN SALES CULTURE. DATA TRUMPS INTUITION.

Dave Elkington

CHAPTER 18

MQL VS SQL

To better prepare yourself for what might be coming, here the major friction point that likely come to light when such a meeting takes place between sales and marketing.

"LEADS" this is the word. We all know that generating leads is crucial for businesses, but not all leads are created equal.

According to statistic, sales teams that receive higher quality leads have better conversion rates, but 61% of B2B marketers send all their leads to sales, even though only 27% are qualified.

Not enough Information Qualified Leads (IQLs) or Marketing Qualified Leads (MQLs).

These leads appear at the top of the sales lifecycle. IQLs are those that give contact details such as a name or email address - in exchange for valuable content, such as e-book, whitepapers or custom videos.

Meanwhile, MQLs include the same thing but are from people who have responded positively to a presented material such as a blog, a video, a webinar, or a slide deck.

It's important to distinguish that MQLs are not necessarily ready to speak to a salesperson, but are still considering options and evaluating the market. The goal of an MQL from a marketing perspective is to present them with opportunities to advance to a sales qualified lead (SQL) lifecycle stage.

Not enough Sales Qualified Leads (SQLs).

These are the leads that are the equivalent of shooting fish in a barrel. They are at the end of the sales lifecycle and are ready to buy and are reaching out to contact your firm to initiate the transaction.

Too many unqualified SQLs. They are either incorrectly called SQLs or are not as firm as they are thought to be.

Not many repeat customers (low churn rate).

For example:

First scenario: Marketing has the idea to create a whitepaper that 5,000 people download for free. However, 2,500 of these people are not decision makers, and 2,300 of them do not have the money to purchase any services. In this scenario we have a low MQL to SQL conversion rate of 4% puts the onus of change on the marketing department.

Second Scenario: Marketing creates the same whitepaper, limits its distribution behind a paywall and an information grab, giving out the initial link only to management level and higher contacts from niche message boards. Only 500 people download the whitepaper now. However, sales drops the ball and converts only 2 of these customers. This 0.4% SQL to MQL factor should mean trouble for the sales department, not marketing.

These are some of the most common points of friction for sales and marketing departments regardless of whether they are merging or not. The coming together of sales and marketing can solve a lot of these issues.

The first things is to clarify the MQL to SQL process and let your sales and marketing groups team up on and align on the customer experience, nurturing and presenting valuable content that leads the prospect further down the sales lifecycle.
They can combine to create content that answers common questions asked by bottom-of-the-sales-cycle qualifiers. It's essential to create content and campaigns that are relevant to specific stages in the buying process, and a software automation can play a crucial part in this because we have to

ensure the customer's experience is seamless, connected and contextual every step of the way — from MQL to SQL to close.

Harvard Review article lists that 80% of collateral produced by marketing departments goes unused. But at the time, many marketing departments are unfamiliar with what a good lead looks like. Sales can help make define the different types of leads to get all content moving in the same direction to appeal to a certain type of qualifier. This is one of the reasons Sales and Marketing should get on the same page.

Set up time with your sales leaders to get their input on lead quality and what converts to revenue. Understanding their process once a lead is assigned to them will help you know how a prospect is handled at every stage of the sales lifecycle.

First the Sales must define what a good lead looks like and bad lead looks like.

Second discuss what actions a lead has to take to become an MQL.

Third document the process after an MQL is passed over to Sales to help identify gaps in the sales follow-up process.

When all is said and done, aligned goals are the base of an effective sales and marketing alliance. Aligning the goals of marketing and sales teams starts with connecting the data that they analyze. Consider the types of data that provide insights into marketing efforts rather than sales developments.

Enhance communication between teams setting aside time on a monthly basis to meet and collaborate on lead generation goals, this can help to increase effectiveness and efficiency for both departments.

IF YOU ARE NOT TAKING CARE
OF YOUR CUSTOMER, YOUR
COMPETITOR WILL.

Bob Hooey

CHAPTER 19

CUSTOMER RETENTION

Merging the Marketing and Sales is not only useful for customer acquisition. We are well aware that a loyal customer is worth much more than a new customer. After we spend a lot of time and resources to acquire a customer our goal is to retain as many and much as possible, because it's one of the most worthy investments a business can make.

Like we mentioned before in chapter 7 the traditional sales funnel are complete inadequate today. There is no consideration of the conversation you are having with your leads or the alignment of the salesperson has with your marketing narrative, and this is reflected in a lack of consideration about the loyalty stage, that generate a limited or absence of post-purchase effects.

Here's the problem: companies drive customers away with poor customer retention initiatives, and it is here that a Sales and Marketing integration look to make positive impacts with ideas like loyalty schemes, customer follow-ups, and reward programs.

Here some figures about customer retention:

- You're 40% more likely to sell to a past customer than to gain a new one.
- Loyal customers spend up to 30% more than new leads.
- The probability of successfully selling to a past customer is almost 70%, while sales success among new leads ranges from 5 to 20%.
- Loyal customers are 50% more willing to try a new product of yours, than would new customers.

Where to start?

To improve understanding of your customers and how they arrive at your brand, your sales and marketing teams need to work side by side, sharing information.

Your sales department can provide very useful data from the field about profiles of the average interested customer, helping to draw conclusions on how best to approach them, where to locate them, and which competing brands might be of interest to them.

We can start to analyze which factors influence the buying decision of the customers you've already gained, and which journey of discovery most often serves to attract them to your brand, in order to improve your success and retention ratio.

You won't be able to keep 100% of your customers. Some will fall off due to reasons outside of your control, or simply because they no longer need your product or service. However, you can dramatically increase customer retention by applying these 4 basic strategies:

THE MOST OBVIOUS WAY TO ENSURE CUSTOMER RETENTION IS TO PREVENT A CUSTOMER FROM LEAVING

You will need to analyze the "warning" signal, to identify the key variables, like purchase pattern, product usage, and service enquiries. These data can be collected from Sales team, Service team, and historical information into the CRM.

WE NEED TO CONSTANTLY BUILD TRUST

Showing more customer appreciation, that you care about them and you're thankful for their business. We need to start from a thank you email, for example, to confirm they have received their service or product, and ask them if they have any question of feedback.

The feedback itself can contain an amount of untold information that can help you to improve your product and services. And drafting a trend within the customer feedback you can have the sense of what the customer want most.

You can start asking them one simple survey question: "On a scale of 0 to 10, how likely are you to recommend this company's product or service to a friend or a colleague?"

A continue proactive interaction with your customer allow you to anticipate their wants, needs, and next moves, and try to handle potential problems before they pop up.

In addition these information are useful to improve your customer personas and map out their wants and needs, so you can improve your depth blog posts, how-to guides, actionable content, Instagram pictures, LinkedIn slide deck ...

YOU CAN CREATE CUSTOMER LOYALTY PROGRAMS

offering small incremental discount, free features, upgrades or rewards. You can provide them exclusive products or deals or free shipping. Again a CRM software lets you view a customer's purchase history, so that you can determine what kind of offer will be the most appealing, and the Sales team has additional information about the sales process that can reveal what the customer is really keen to have or maintain.

KEEP YOUR BRAND PROMISES

Keeping your promises is the ultimate sign of professionalism in business. This kind of marketing will help you build a better relationship with customers and keep them coming back to you as a resource. Make your buyers feel informed, cared and keep to meet their expectations so they are keen to remain with your brand.

Another important factor is the brand image, based on good communication and digital content, is essential nowadays and can enhance the perceived image of your products that could become more important than their real value (which explains the consumer loyalty with certain brand like Apple or Tesla).

You can do much more depend of the sector where you are in or product or services that you are selling, like Social Responsibly Program, onboarding program, Newsletter, education program etc. The main takeaway on this process is your marketing and sales team works together to deliver a personalised seamless experience between your brand and your product.

THE NEW REALITY IS THAT SALES AND MARKETING ARE CONTINUOUSLY AND INCREASINGLY INTEGRATED. MARKETING NEEDS TO KNOW MORE ABOUT SALES, SALES NEEDS TO KNOW MORE ABOUT MARKETING, AND WE ALL NEED TO KNOW MORE ABOUT OUR CUSTOMERS.

Jill Rowley

CHAPTER 20

MBS: THE DEATH OF SALES FUNNEL

Like we have seen in the chapter 7 the sales funnel in based on the AIDA principle and in order to close more sales it's all about keeping a steady flow of prospects in the various stages of the funnel. As you close some, others are entering the next stage, ready for your full attention to be cast on them.

The top of the funnel includes the new opportunities. As they enter the funnel, they must travel through the various aspects of the funnel, until they get to the bottom, which is the close. The way leads travel through the funnel is by constantly qualifying and managing the opportunity, and ultimately determining if there's a need for your solution.

The cost of your sale determines how quickly your deal passes through the funnel. For example, if your average deal is $5,000, it might move through the funnel fairly quickly, because you don't need as many signatures. But if you have a deal worth $100,000, it will take longer to move through the funnel because it will require several proposals, presentations, and a lot more decision makers will need to get involved. All of this will slow the deal down, and give it a longer lifespan. If you want to close more deals, you need to fill your funnel with lots of prospects and leads. Some sales organizations have an established marketing engine that distributes leads into the top of the funnel. Once you take the time to call these leads, there are some that will materialize. These are the ones that will enter your sales funnel.

That traditional type of funnel, which you've been using for decades in your marketing and sales to generate traffic and then convert and close leads into customers, is dead. Why is it dead? Because the funnel uses a linear approach.

Let me explain.

The problem with most companies is that they were built with your dad in mind, rather than you. In yesterday's world where customers' main source of information was their vendors, you thought of your business like a funnel. But in a world where customers' main source of information is other customers, you cannot continue to use a traditional funnel where the loyalty stage, a phase to built trust and gained referrals, is not even considered like part of the process.

If you want to grow better in 2020, you need to match your business to the modern buyer, throw away the funnel and embrace the MBS.

In the past, marketers followed a communication model called AIDA. The acronym stood for awareness, interest, desire, and action. So, what's missing in the AIDA model? The customer experience.

The sales funnel based on the AIDA model is limited due to the absence of post-purchase effects such as satisfaction, consumption, referrals, etc. This model is also limited by its reliance on the concept of a linear, hierarchical response process. Indeed, some research suggests that consumers process promotional information via dual pathways, namely both cognitive (thinking) and affective (feeling) simultaneously.

The three major issues during a sales journey using AIDA model are:

First: We can't truly and accurately predict where a lead is located. Your lead could be ready to buy, or they could be months away from buying. It's their decision, not yours, on how and where they should spend their money.

Second: I consistently see one of the most important stages left off all sales funnels, which is the loyalty stage. Maintaining a good relationship is a way to encourage customers to tell others about your product or service and generate referrals.

Third: The metrics and KPIs concerning stages of the sales funnel are complete inadequate today. There is no consideration of the conversation you are having with your leads or the alignment of the salesperson has with your marketing narrative.

The sales funnel really gives companies, and executive teams, the wrong idea of who is buying from them. Always remember that a human is buying from us. Not a percentage. Not a robot. Not a "conversion ratio." A human, in the end.

So it is the customer experience that determines the success of your business, not an algorithm or a formula that you plug full of numbers based on every client's choices.

The fundamental problem with the funnel is that it shows the customers as an output. That switch has been flipped to where customers nowadays are an input. In addition, the beginning of the buying process has changed. It's word-of-mouth that now drives the majority of new customers. Said that the death of the funnel is not the end of sales and marketing. Just as they do with soft sales skills, just need to adjust their energy and release it in a much more efficient way.

Here is the breakdown of the MBS:

Once the customer is in your MBS process, you can't forget about them. Instead, you have to take care of them. This is accomplished by following up with contacts, presenting your business plans to them and moving them along the customer's journey until you eventually reach the close.

The important thing about the MBS and closing deals is to always be moving multiple clients through the various stages in the sales cycle. You need to keep your eye on every deal as it travels through the sales stages, which neatly align with your prospect's buying cycle. A healthy MBS has a good mix of prospects at different levels in the buying process. Some may be at the beginning, needing further qualification. Some are in the middle, where you've already had some contacts. Others may sit at the decision stage, where you're waiting for a response on a proposal or a quote. And don't forget the loyalty stage, where your business is maintaining the relationship.

Your ability to build, manage, and maintain a healthy MBS is the key to routinely closing sales. Your long-term survival absolutely depends on it. So with all that in mind, think about your sales process. What does it look like right now, and what isn't it doing that it should do? Are your Sales and Marketing aligned?

Blending your sales and marketing teams is a fantastic way to grow your business and scale it beyond what separate sales and marketing teams are capable of, in addition by moving sales and marketing into a single department, you'll be able to uncover unique insights into the sales process, fine-tune and optimize your sales and marketing strategies, as well as grow new business opportunities and increase revenues.

A fully aligned, hybrid sales and marketing team puts your organization in the best position to extract the most value from prospects and customers. This will be a foundation that leads to growing your business to new heights.

This is what I call MBS: M like Marketing, S for Sales and the Buyer in the middle.

However, sales and marketing alignment is no easy feat. It requires an investment in both time and resources from all involved parties and coming together on a regular basis to discuss goals, communicate concerns, and most importantly, celebrate successes. By utilizing the tips for marketing and sales alignment as stated in this book, these two teams can formulate a strong sales and marketing strategy that incorporates the strengths of both teams, using up-to-date, information and content to their advantage.

SO, WHAT TO DO NOW?

Do you have your marketing plan? What is your alignment plan? How your sales deliver your message? I believe all these need to become an essential part of any business plan, something that everyone intend to succeed must draft.

There is no doubt that this book could have easily been five times longer and that each chapter could have been filled with more detailed research and even more information and examples. I challenged myself to write the shortest BIG book I could, something full of practical information with no padding and nothing extra. Anything missing at this point is for you to figure out while on the journey and if you need help to engineer or optimize your sales and marketing strategy that helps your teams align more fully with what your prospects are searching for, we're here to help.

Subscribe to the FOUNDCOO mailing list to have the step by step MBS worksheet.

www.foundcoo.com

Or you can to get in touch with our team if you need more help.

www.foundcoo.com/request

ABOUT
THE AUTHOR

Mauro Berno is Founder and CEO at FOUNDCOO, a Sales and Marketing transformation firm that helps to reinvent business models, incorporating internally generated success with externally generated innovation. Mauro founded FOUNDCOO with the belief that there's always a smarter and better way to do things, leveraging training to cultivate a high-performance sales culture, developing leadership and coaching skills, and applying more effective organizational design.

As CEO he is constantly pushing the boundaries to rise above outdated, unworkable middle class myths and limitations. He took everything he has learned about business from his previous roles and created a training organization that delivers to people the practical skills they need to attain the success they are looking for. His vast knowledge and experience can be simplified into two main areas: Acquiring more customers and Having them come back more often.

To schedule and learn more about MBS, e-mail info@foundcoo.com, or visit www.foundcoo.com.

To schedule Mauro to speak at your next event, e-mail info@foundcoo.com.

www.ingramcontent.com/pod-product-compliance
Lightning Source LLC
Chambersburg PA
CBHW030616220526
45463CB00004B/1309